Making sense of politics

MAKING SENSE OF POLITICS

Arthur Sanders

Iowa State University Press / Ames

For Debby, who helps me make sense of life

Arthur Sanders is assistant professor of political science at Drake University, Des Moines, Iowa.

Chapter 1 epigram reprinted from "The Ladder" by Prince, © 1985 Controversy Music. All rights on behalf of Controversy Music for the U.S.A. and Canada only. All rights reserved. Used by permission.

Portions of Chapter 2 reprinted from Arthur Sanders, "Ideological Symbols," *American Politics Quarterly* 17, no. 3 (July 1989):227–55.

Chapter 4 epigram reprinted from "My Hometown" by Bruce Springsteen, © 1984 Bruce Springsteen. Used by permission.

Chapter 4 epigram reprinted from "America" by Paul Simon, © 1968 Paul Simon. Used by permission.

Chapter 5 epigram reprinted from "Peace, Love, and Understanding" by Nick Lowe, © 1982 Plangent Visions Music Inc. Used by permission.

Chapter 8 epigram from "Twisted" by Annie Ross and Wardell Gray, © 1965 Prestige Music. Used by permission.

First edition, 1990

Library of Congress Cataloging-in-Publication Data

Sanders, Arthur
    Making sense of politics / Arthur Sanders. — 1st ed.
    p.   cm.
    Includes bibliographical references (p.).
    ISBN 0–8138–0301–2
    1. Public opinion — United States.   I. Title.
HN90.P8S26   1990
303.3′8′0973 — dc20
                            90–33581

Contents

Acknowledgments

Working on this book has been challenging, time-consuming, and, above all else, enjoyable. If it is a worthy project, that is no doubt due to the help and support I received. I would first like to thank the twenty-six people I interviewed for this project. They remain, as I promised, anonymous, but without them this book would not have been possible. More important, their willingness to talk openly and freely with me made my job fun. I looked forward to my interviews, and I was rarely disappointed. I would recommend that anyone interested in the study of public opinion spend some time actually talking to people about politics. It is an eye-opening experience.

Hamilton College and the American Political Science Association provided financial support for the project, and for that too, I am grateful. Additionally, Hamilton provided me with a leave in the fall of 1987 in order to work on the manuscript. And June Darrow, our very efficient and helpful department secretary, aided me in contacting prospective interviewees, for which she deserves much thanks.

My colleagues, past and present, in the Hamilton College government department have listened to me talk about my work, and they have always been receptive, insightful, and helpful. In particular, I would like to thank Frank Anecharico, Deborah Gerner, and Michael Mastanduno for their help in clarifying my thinking at various stages of this project. Henry Rutz, of the Hamilton College anthropology department, provided helpful comments on an early draft of the book. Ken Wagner, a former member of the sociology department at Hamilton, deserves thanks as well; we spent many a long evening talking about politics and public opinion, and my ideas on the subject are much richer as a result.

I would like to thank my parents, Saul and Ellie Sanders, for their help and support over the years. Without their encouragement, love, and guidance, I would never have been in a position to pursue an academic career in the first place.

I also would like to thank the 1974–78 government department of Franklin and Marshall College, especially Bob Gray, Stanley Michalak, Dick Schier, Grier Stephenson, and Sid Wise. These individuals showed me what it was to be a teacher-scholar, and they encouraged me to pursue my goal of a doctorate in political science.

The people at Iowa State University Press have made my work on this book as pleasant as possible. They have all been helpful, accessible, and easy to work with, especially my editors Gretchen Van Houten and Rosemary Sheffield. They have responded to all my questions and straightened out many problems. I could not ask for a better publisher.

Sidney Verba read the entire manuscript, and his comments and suggestions were, as always, extremely useful. I wrote my dissertation under his supervision seven years ago, but it is his continued help, guidance, and support for which I am most grateful. All of my work has benefited from his wisdom, and this book is no exception.

Finally, and most important, my wife, Deborah Pappenheimer, deserves more thanks than I can describe. She listened to my ideas, talked with me at length about the book, read the manuscript, and helped me keep this project (and my life) in perspective. She has my everlasting love, and I have dedicated this book to her.

Making sense of politics

Introduction

Everybody's looking 4 the answers
How the story started and how it will end

—PRINCE

Laura Rivers is a sixty-four-year-old grandmother. Her husband died ten years ago, and she went to work in the family store at that time. She retired last year and now lives on savings and social security. She has a high school education, and she describes her interest in politics as limited. When I asked her why her interest was so limited, she replied:

I'm not knowledgeable. I mean I think you have to work at it. You got to be up on things and say it. If you don't know what you are talking about, better you keep your mouth shut.

*And why do you think you are not knowledgeable?**

Too many other things to do. The days aren't long enough anymore. Like now I'm a wife, mother, and grandmother. I got three granddaughters next door. And I have a full day. Busy with my church, and fundraising activities, and I'm afraid politics would be the lesser. I don't make it a hobby. What I read in the paper, I try to keep up on it. But some-

---

*The author's questions during interviews are given in *italics* throughout the book.

times things are above my head. Like the magazine, *Ms.* — I discontinued it. And they said, "Why?" And I said, "It's all over my head. You write things that I can't even comprehend." I suppose if I ran to a dictionary I could, but I was getting no pleasure out of it. And I think that's what would be with politics.

Still, Laura often votes, although not always, and she does try to come to grips with the world around her. Laura tries to make sense of politics.

In many ways, Laura's dilemma is a common one. Most people, as we know, do not give politics and public affairs a high priority in their lives, so sorting out political events can be difficult. But even people with a great deal of interest often must struggle to understand the political world. For example, Simon Pinella is a twenty-five-year-old college graduate. He is a professional with a good income, and he follows politics and political news regularly. When I asked him about U.S. policy in Central America,[1] he replied:

> I think that's one of the neglected areas that I don't know very much about. And I probably fall in the class of Americans that don't know much about it, so you don't concern yourself too much with it. And I think what I hear coming from some of those countries is deplorable. But it kind of comes in waves, and you don't hear something for a while and you forget about it. It slips out of your mind. But like we mined Nicaragua's harbors, I think it was. You know, the reason behind it really isn't clear in my mind. And I think we're never presented with a picture of the other side here. I think that's some of the United States propaganda. I haven't been informed on what the Nicaraguans think, and why are they against the United States? Even though we hear bits and pieces, it's different from talking to somebody down there.

Making sense of politics is not easy. As in Laura's case, many of us have better things to do with our time. And as in Simon's case, even when we do have an interest, it is not possible to understand and follow everything that goes on. There will be gaps in the information we have at our disposal.

However, even a brief conversation with the least interested and least involved people will quickly make clear that just about everyone does try, at least minimally, to make some sense of politics. It is a topic that may not interest us much, but it is hard to get away from it entirely, and people will try to understand the information they do have. People like to feel they have some idea about how the world in which they live operates. The question then is, How do people attempt to make sense of the world of politics? How do they understand what they see, and how do they evaluate the information that they do have in order to make decisions about politics?

In our democracy, we rely on the opinions of the people to guide policy, at least in a broad sense. At a minimum, we allow the public to choose our leaders. At a maximum, we expect our leaders to do exactly what the public wants. But in trying to understand public opinion, we are often confounded by an inability to understand what it is that people desire. Throughout the Reagan years, for example, we have faced the seeming paradox that people respond positively to the president while disapproving of many of his policies. How are analysts or, more important, our elected leaders supposed to interpret such a paradox? Is the public indifferent to policy positions, or does it judge policy and leadership by different standards? And if the latter is true, can leaders follow public wishes on policy? No single study can answer all of these questions, but we at least need to make some sense of how people think about the political world. A better understanding of people's sense of politics will give us a clearer view of the potentials and limitations of democracy.

Fortunately, we do not need to start this study from scratch. Political scientists have shed light on the answers to these questions. We know, for example, that people do not think about politics in an ideological manner.[2] But even after many years of intensive study, there is still much that we do not know. This book is an attempt to probe these questions more fully.

The shape of public opinion

Trying to understand how people think about politics has been a growing issue in political science for the past twenty-five to thirty years.[3] We have spent an enormous amount of time and effort studying and modeling the ways that people make sense of politics. Yet, as Sniderman and Tetlock note, "The more we learn about public opinion, the less apparent is its basis of organization."[4]

Still, we have learned some things. We know, for example, that most people do not spend a lot of time thinking about politics; politics is a low priority for most members of the general public. As a result, most people do not know a lot about politics. The public often seems ignorant of simple political facts. For example, two out of three people do not know the term of office of a United States senator,[5] and in 1980 only 15 percent of a national sample could correctly identify the Democrats as having retained control of the House of Representatives.[6] It is also clear that most people do not think about politics in an ideological fashion: They do not have clear, consistent, constrained belief systems.[7] As Kinder and Sears note, most Americans are characterized by "ideological innocence."[8]

Yet we know that most Americans do make political decisions and evaluations. They vote. They respond to particular political figures. As Kinder and Sears put it, "Innocent though Americans may typically be of ideological principles, they are hardly innocent of political ideas."[9] The question then is, How do Americans think about politics? What are the factors that guide their ideas and thoughts about political issues and people?

Unfortunately, Kinder and Sears also note, "We now know rather more about how Americans do *not* think about politics than about how they do."[10] Part of the problem in figuring out how people think about politics is an overreliance on a single form of analysis: survey research. Survey research is an incredibly useful and powerful tool that allows us to study large numbers of people and, from those samples, make generalizations about the general population. It has also proved to be relatively cost-effective and efficient. Large organizations, such as the Center for Political Studies at the University of Michigan or the National Opinion Research Council at the University of Chicago, can undertake extensive surveys and make their results available to a wide range of scholars. And the pressure for productivity among college faculty makes it attractive to use data collected by others as the basis for books and articles.

However, survey research has its limitations. Most important, it is difficult in a survey interviewing situation to delve deeply into the thoughts that people have. As Tony Hunter, a thirty-eight-year-old manual laborer with two years of college, said to me:

> I was wondering if you were going to ask yes-and-no, true-and-false. You don't find anything out that way. And a lot of these polls are that way. "Do you believe this? Yes or no? True or false? One of the above." They're answering the question for you by saying that. Yes-or-no—that don't mean nothing. And I don't think they give these people time enough to think. And some of these questions they ask, I'd have to stop and think. I'm sure in these polls they call on the phone or something, and they're not going to wait five or ten minutes. Some of these questions they've asked people, I'd have to think five minutes about, unless I had been thinking about that or been involved or such.

Similarly, the need to conduct a large number of interviews in a relatively short time means we often do not follow up to find out what people mean by the responses they give. And the need to ask the same questions of all individuals means we may not even ask people about the things that matter to them. If we want to understand how people make sense of the world of politics, we need to spend more time talking to people about that world.

I am not arguing that survey research is meaningless or unimportant. On the contrary, we can learn things from survey research that we cannot learn in any other way. But there needs to be more emphasis on other types of research techniques if we are to understand public opinion fully. In fact, our use of survey research will improve if we supplement it with other methodologies. We will be better able to interpret the results that we do see, and we will have a better sense of the types of questions we need to ask if we want to understand the dynamics of opinion.

This book is an attempt at just such a study. It is the result of a series of twenty-five extended discussions with citizens that attempts to sort out how they try to make sense of the political world. By using in-depth interviews to understand people's ideas more fully, this study is not unique. It is undertaken in the tradition of Robert Lane and Jennifer Hochschild.[11] Those studies, in particular Lane's work on ideology, have found that people try to make sense of the world around them, although their sense of it may not be sophisticated and they may not connect all of their views together in a consistent way (to use Lane's term, they "morselize" opinions).[12] Politics may be distant and unimportant, but it is not totally ignored. Where the present study differs from these previous studies, however, is in its emphasis on how people think about contemporary issues and leaders.

I was not particularly interested in larger issues of justice and ideology, though as we will see, these larger issues are important in helping people sort out politics. Rather, I undertook these interviews with the objective of discovering how people made sense of politics in the here and now. How do they sort out the variety of issues and leaders that are present in the contemporary political scene? What categories or principles do they use to evaluate politicians and policies? This book, then, is an attempt to understand the process by which people understand politics in contemporary America, and the chapters that follow document how political opinions are organized. We will explore the factors that seem to set the parameters of people's political ideas and are central to the worldview that these people hold. And we will, in the end, show how the information obtained from these in-depth discussions can supplement and improve our use of survey research. But before exploring the interviews, I want to introduce the individuals I talked with.

The sample

During the summer and fall of 1986, I undertook a series of twenty-five in-depth interviews with a group of randomly selected citizens of the Utica, New York, area.[13] The interviews were designed to explore the way that people think about politics, focusing on the kinds of things that people believe are important and how they make sense of political events, people, and issues.

Individuals were chosen at random from the Utica telephone directory. They were contacted by mail and asked if they were willing to participate in the project. I was able to offer them twenty-five dollars as compensation for their time, and I had to contact sixty-two people in order to get twenty-five respondents. (Note that during the twenty-five interviews, I actually talked to twenty-six people. The husband of one of the women I talked to was home doing chores around the house during our conversation, and he involved himself in the conversation quite frequently. Rather than ignore his views, I have included him as a separate respondent.) The interviews, which were recorded on tape, ranged in length from about an hour and twenty minutes to three hours and forty minutes. The interviewees were promised anonymity; hence the names used here are fictitious. The given names were chosen at random from a list of names in a baby-name book, and the surnames were chosen at random from a list of the world champion 1977 and 1978 New York Yankees baseball teams. Other demographic details have also been changed to protect anonymity.

Each of the respondents was asked a number of standard demographic and political questions. The questions on interest, party identification, and ideological identification, and a few others, were the standard Center for Political Studies questions on these topics. Appendix C lists the standard political questions that were asked of each individual to allow some comparability between this group and the general population.

In order to make the interviews as objective as possible, I tried whenever I could, to have at least two days off between interviews, and I tried to put each interview out of my mind as I went on to the next one. The point was not to ask questions that would elicit responses that fit into particular patterns but to allow individuals to express themselves as freely as possible without my leading them in any particular way. It was only after I had finished all of the interviews that I began listening to the tapes and thinking about them. I spent close to six months simply listening to the conversations and making notes about my impressions before I began to think systematically about what had been said.

The group I talked to was quite diverse, as can be seen in

Appendix A, and was fairly representative of the population in terms of interest, education, and age (the proportion of senior citizens is in line with figures from the Utica area). Additionally, the political characteristics (vote turnout in 1984, vote choice in 1984, party identification, and ideological self-identification) reflect those of the region. Three qualities of the response group as a whole, however, require brief comment.

First, the group was heavily Catholic. This reflects the makeup of the area. Utica is a declining industrial city (it has been declining since the 1950s) with a heavily Catholic (especially Italian American) ethnic population.

Second, all of the respondents were Caucasian. This, again, is not surprising, given the small size of the black and Hispanic populations in Utica, but it does mean we should be particularly careful in this regard. It is clear, for example, that blacks and whites have different perspectives on politics in a number of areas, including the role of government and the causes of inequality.[14] The different experiences of minority groups in America may lead them to think about politics in very different ways.

Third, the response set was disproportionately male. This results, I believe, from two factors. First, single women are more likely to have unlisted phone numbers, eliminating them from my sample set. Second, many married couples have their phone number listed in the husband's name, so my original letters were more likely to be addressed to the husband. (See Appendix D for a copy of the letter sent to each household.) Although the letter said I would like to talk to "an adult member of the household," there was some tendency for the person to whom the letter was addressed to feel that he or she was the one I should talk to.

Still, the eight women I interviewed constituted a broad and diverse group. They included both the youngest (age twenty) and the oldest (age eighty) people I talked to. Two were married, two were single, two were divorced, and two were widows. The women did not seem, as a group, to be very different in the way they thought about things from the men I talked with. Thus, although they were not representative of the gender distribution in the population, I am not particularly concerned that this has created a bad mix in the group I interviewed.

Finally, it is clear that a group willing to take the time to talk with me may, by that reason alone, be unrepresentative of the general population. Thus, applying my results to the general population may be useless. Having spent a lot of time talking with these people, I am confident this was not the case. Their reasons for participating in the project varied. A small minority did it because they enjoy talking about politics. A few did it out of curiosity, including one college student home for the summer and one Hamilton College alumnus who wanted to see what was going on at the campus. Most, however, did it for the money, some because they needed it badly (in particular two people who were unemployed and one who was on welfare) and some because it seemed like an easy way to get a little extra spending money. The group, as will be clear, was not by any measure a political elite. Only four respondents had ever undertaken any political activity at all, and a fair number of them professed great or almost total ignorance of political events and issues. (Still, as it became clear upon questioning them, even those who were largely ignorant of what was happening tried to make sense of those things they heard about or knew about.)

Let me take a moment to introduce these people to you. I have grouped them by level of education.

Of the twenty-six people, three had only a grade school education. (See Appendix B for a summary of each of the people I talked with.) Nancy Gullet, a seventy-nine-year-old widow, immigrated to this country with her family and settled in the Utica area shortly after World War I. She worked in the mills until the birth of her first child and remained a housewife afterward. Of all the people I talked with, Nancy probably was the least informed about and the least interested in politics.

Dave Thomasson was a seventy-seven-year-old veteran of World War II who was still working part-time at a local retail store. Married with three children, Dave was also a poet. He brought a number of his poems with him to the interview and read some of those dealing with political topics to me. Still, Dave did not take an active interest in politics.

The third individual with only a grade school education was Carla Zeber. A sixty-seven-year-old housewife, Carla had often been involved in local community organizations, but not in anything she was willing to describe as political. Although she had worked as a government employee for twenty-three years, she thought of herself primarily as a homemaker. She was one of the eight Protestants I talked with.

Three other individuals had some high school experience but had never received a high school degree. Gail Blair was a fifty-year-old divorcée who had worked as an unskilled laborer but was now collecting a full-disability pension from the state. Her interest in politics ran hot and cold. There were times in her life when she followed what was happening and took at least enough interest to vote, and other periods when she did not. At the time of the interview, she said she was beginning to follow what was happening for the first time in about ten years.

Howard Gossage was sixty-eight years old and had only a limited interest in politics. At the time we talked, the issue that seemed to consume him was that the State of New York was issuing new license plates with the Statue of Liberty on them when, according to him, no one knew whether the statue actually was in New York or New Jersey (he brought this up three times in the course of our conversation). Howard had worked as a manual laborer for most of his life but was now retired. He was married and had four children.

Third, was Gus White, a fifty-three-year-old unemployed manual laborer. Gus had recently been laid off after working in his field for thirty-five years. He was on his second marriage, and he had little interest in politics. Of those I talked to, Gus was one of the least interested and least informed about politics, but that lack of interest sprang from a deep alienation from the political process.

Five of the people I interviewed had high school degrees but no further education. Sue Doyle was a thirty-four-year-old housewife with one child. Sue had worked in business until the birth of her child. She quit her job at that time to become a full-time housewife (something she believed was the correct thing to do), but now that her child was of school age, she found time to work part-time. Still, she believed that mothers should all stay home with their children and not work. Sue did not have much interest in politics, but she was relatively well informed. She paid attention to what happened, but politics was a low-priority concern.

On the other hand, Carl Figueroa, a thirty-five-year-old manual laborer, was one of the two most politically involved people I talked with. Carl had worked on a few campaigns, both nationally and locally. He was single, a Protestant, and a union member. In spite of his union membership, however, he was a strong Republican, and, in fact, he thought that a major problem with unions was their partisanship. Although he had never served in Vietnam, his interest in politics developed from an interest in that conflict, which he believed "we could have won": "We could have won, but we didn't. It's too bad." He followed international affairs more closely than anyone else I talked with.

Martha Nettles, fifty-two years old, had been separated from her husband for a number of years and had four children. She worked as a secretary and had a good deal of interest in politics, though she was quick to admit that politics made her "feel helpless." But Martha had an abiding faith that in the end, all would work out for the best because all of life was part of God's plan.

Ralph Randolph had dropped out of high school in the tenth grade but later earned his equivalency degree. Ralph was a manual laborer in the construction trade but was unemployed at the time of our discussion. He was twenty-eight years old, was married with one child, and often found it necessary to travel south in the winter to find work. Ralph had never voted, though in the previous year he had registered for the first time. He said his interest in politics was quite limited, but he watched the news and read the paper regularly, and he had a relatively clear sense of what was happening in politics.

The fifth, was Laura Rivers, who was mentioned at the beginning of this chapter. Laura also regularly read the paper and watched the news on television, but like Ralph, she had only a limited interest in politics. She did have a collection of cartoons on her refrigerator, a number of which had political themes (and were clearly old enough that I knew they had not simply been put up for my perusal). Laura had spent most of her life as a housewife but went to work in the family retail business when her husband died, a job she worked at for a dozen years before she retired. She had three children and five grandchildren. Of Lebanese ancestry, she was a Maronite Catholic, a heritage of which she was very proud.

Six individuals had some college education but no bachelor's degree. However, two of these people, Adam Clay and Amy

Tidrow, were still in college. Adam was a twenty-year-old student who had just finished his sophomore year and was home for the summer. He had a limited interest in politics. Amy, also twenty, was in the process of earning her second associate's degree at the local community college and was planning to go on for her B.A. When I asked what her religion was, she said she was "Independent" (though she had been raised "just Protestant"). She had a moderate interest in politics, though she said her schoolwork plus the part-time job she held to pay for her schooling made it difficult for her to find the time to follow what was happening.

Walter Beattie, the only Jewish person I interviewed, was a fifty-six-year-old with an associate's degree. Walter was married with two children and had been a white-collar worker at the same firm for more than thirty years. He did not pay much attention to politics, and he said that though he read the paper daily, "you read it and forget it." Although he told me, "I like to be led—I am not good at coming up with my own comments," he managed to talk to me for well over two hours.

Mark Dent, a thirty-nine-year-old manual laborer, was one of the two Vietnam veterans I talked with. Married with two children, Mark said, "The big lesson I got out of [my experience in Vietnam] was to learn to think for myself. Check out everything that you can, and then make your own decision. Because I never even really knew why I was there." That attitude was indicative of a deep cynicism. In fact, before he would agree to the interview, I had to assure him that I was not working for the government in an attempt to find out what people thought in case they had to be "rounded up" someday.

George Heath, fifty-nine, had retired a couple of years earlier after working as a government employee for more than thirty years. George had been active in local politics in his younger days, but his involvement had diminished now that "all of my close friends [in local politics] are gone anyways." He had worked for the local Democratic Party (though not for any national-level candidates), and his interest in politics remained strong. He followed national and local events closely.

Last was Tony Hunter, thirty-eight, a manual laborer who had served in the Navy in Vietnam. Tony, like Mark, had developed some interest in politics as a result of his experiences in Vietnam, but he did not have Mark's deep cynicism, even though he noted, "It still baffles me why we were over there." Tony was married and had three children.

Another six of my interviewees were college graduates without any additional degrees. Al Chambliss was a forty-year-old man in small business who had a wife and two children. A political science major in college, Al had a strong interest in politics, though he never had been active in politics in any way. Al believed strongly in the abilities of "science" to provide us information about people. Thus, he advocated greater use of techniques such as handwriting analysis, lie detectors, and the study of people's skull size and shape to provide information about politicians.

John Guidry, twenty-seven, was married with no children and worked as a traveling salesperson for a national company. He had a degree in accounting and was somewhat interested in politics. He was the one person I talked to who said he got most of his information about politics on the radio. He was on the road a lot and relied on radio call-in and talk shows for political news and analysis.

Clyde Lyle was twenty-four years old and married with no children. When I spoke with him, he had just graduated from college with a degree in computer science, and was looking for work. He said he had only some interest in politics. On the other hand, he followed political news fairly closely, on television, in the newspaper, and in magazines. He was the only person to volunteer that he also got political information from discussions with friends.

Simon Pinella had earned a degree in engineering two years earlier and worked in a white-collar position for a local company. He was twenty-five years old and single. Simon's father was a shop steward in a union and a strong Democrat, but Simon supported Republicans and did not like unions (they were useful, but their day had passed, he said). He was interested in politics and followed it regularly. However, he had never gotten very involved and sometimes did not even vote. That made him "feel a little ashamed." He said, "It upsets [me] that I don't get more involved."

Ed Stanley, thirty-three years old, had a degree in finance. A white-collar worker, he was married with "one child and two dogs." He was very interested in politics, and when I spoke with him, he was about to start working for a candidate for the state assembly in his district, someone he was excited about. Although he had never worked for a candidate before, his parents, especially his mother, had been actively involved in politics.

Sixth was Carol Torrez, an eighty-year-old retired school-teacher. Carol was single and expressed only moderate interest in politics. On the other hand, she had taught social studies in the Utica school system for more than forty years before her retirement, and thus, she noted that she "used to have an intense interest" in things political. That interest had, however, waned in recent years. In fact, when I first contacted her, she sent back the reply card saying she did not want to participate because she no longer paid much attention to politics and I probably would not want to talk to someone like that. Only after I got back in touch with her and reassured her that I was interested in talking with her did she agree to the interview.

Finally, there were three individuals with advanced degrees. Bert Jackson was a forty-year-old professional with a medical degree. Bert was married with one child, and he was by far the most talkative person I met with. A single question from me resulted in a response long enough to fill six or seven single-spaced pages, and our discussion lasted close to four hours. Bert had some interest in politics but was highly cynical about it. He also was cynical about most other things. For example, when I asked him what his religion was, he said:

> I was raised Catholic, and I can't tell you that I am not a Catholic. But I don't practice the religion. . . . I don't hold to the beliefs of any one religion. Because there are things that I just don't agree with in every religion. But I was married in the Catholic Church, and I was baptized. But I go to a Methodist church, and I sit there and listen to the guy, and the guy makes as much sense. . . . I have been to a Presbyterian church, and I sit there and listen, and the Pentecostal church and the Episcopal church. I mean church is church. You do what you got to do. Church is like the Democrats and the Republicans.

Mort Johnson, on the other hand, had a master of divinity degree and was active in his church. Sixty-one years old and a government employee, Mort was married with four children and twelve grandchildren. He was very interested in politics but had never been active in political campaigning of any kind. He was a Republican in his early years, but he said, "In recent years, since World War Two, I have probably voted for more Democrats than Republicans."

Finally, there was Ted Munson, a thirty-four-year-old with a master's degree. Ted was a Protestant and was married with three children. He had only a limited interest in national politics because, as he said, "I don't have much of a belief that what happens nationally politically is going to make that much difference to what happens to me as a citizen of Utica, New York." He did, though, have more of an interest in local politics and had worked briefly in one past mayoral campaign.

These then, were the twenty-six people that I talked to. What follows is an analysis of my conversations with them. In the book, I often refer to the comments of these individuals and, where appropriate, I have reminded the reader of some pertinent facts about each individual. Appendix B lists these individuals alphabetically and provides a summary of the important characteristics (demographic, political, and others) of each.

Chapter 2 explores the role that the common symbols of American politics—the political parties and liberalism and conservativism—play in the thoughts that these people have about politics. These are, after all, the labels and symbols that elites and the media often use to structure their discussions of politics. It is important, therefore, to explore how people relate to and make sense of these symbols. As we shall see, people make sense of these symbols in terms of differences in style and differences in policy. The style-policy distinction developed in Chapter 2 is crucial in sorting out people's visions of the political world. For a minority, politics revolves around "the issues"; support for the proper policy solution is the criterion by which political leaders are judged. For most people, however, politics is a matter of following the proper political style. A leader must be tough or compassionate or diligent. According to this view, good policy results flow from good styles of politics.

Chapters 3 through 5 look at three of the underlying orientations that help structure the way these people think about the political world. Chapter 3 explores the attitudes of trust and distrust that people have toward the political system and our leaders. Chapter 4 looks at the scope of politics, how broadly or narrowly people conceive the political world. Chapter 5, looks at the goals that people have for the political system. All of these factors are basic parameters that shape people's attitudes toward politics.

These underlying orientations are not enough, however, to allow people to make sense of the political world. Chapter 6, then, explores how people use their sense of fairness and their own self-interest to sort through politics. The chapter also examines how people's experiences shape their outlooks on politics and how those experiences often cause people to rely on the politics of style as opposed to the politics of policy.

Chapter 7 turns to the ambiguities and difficulties that people see and have when they think about politics. Although people do think about politics and try to make sense of politics, their world-views often have inconsistencies. In particular, we will focus on the ambiguous attitude that many people have toward democracy itself and how that ambiguity also pushes people toward the politics of style.

Finally, Chapter 8 draws together these various factors and looks more generally at the patterns of political thought that emerge. Again, we will see that some people make sense of politics in terms of issues and policies, but for most, politics is a matter of style. This focus on style is not, however, a focus away from substance. Rather, people who make sense of politics in terms of style are performance-oriented, and style is a way that people can predict future performance. We will also examine some broader survey data in light of what these interviews tell us about the way that people think about politics.

These interviews help give us a clearer sense of how people sort out the political world. They give us a fuller understanding of people's visions of politics in America and how people understand the problems and policies of our nation. They also inform us about how people evaluate leaders and can help us to better understand the dynamics of public opinion in contemporary America.

Signposts of American politics

The starting point for any study of how people make sense of politics is the knowledge that people do not have clear, consistent ideologies.[1] To make sense of the political world, people need to understand the language and symbols that are used by elites and the media to describe and organize that world. In particular, the ideological symbols of liberalism and conservatism and the political parties are common in the discourse of political leaders,[2] and clearly these symbols are familiar to people. As others have noted,[3] about two-thirds of all citizens claim some kind of identification with the symbols of liberalism and conservatism. They can place themselves on the liberal-conservative scale, and there seems to be some link between their self-placement and the policy positions they take. Furthermore, close to 60 percent of the public can give some definition to these words in response to open-ended questions. Although the public is not ideological, ideological identifications do seem to reflect the general political views of many Americans.[4] Similarly, since the publication of *The American Voter,*[5] the importance of party identification for political behavior has been clear. Partisanship seems to contribute to both opinion formation and voting behavior.[6] In this chapter we will look more closely at how people make sense of these symbols and at the ways in which these symbols help people make sense of politics.

Ideological symbols

If liberalism and conservatism do not represent coherent, constrained ideologies, how do they link the ideas that people have? Two possibilities, each of which has some empirical support, suggest themselves. These explanations are not mutually exclusive; each may be present for different segments of the population or even within the same individual.

The first is that people associate these words or symbols with limited sets of issues. That is, people may have narrow views of which policies are central to being a liberal or a conservative. This may cause overall correlations between issue positions and ideological identification to remain low, masking clearer, more refined connections at the individual level.[7] When I used responses to open-ended questions to classify individuals according to the type of issue they associated with the concepts of liberalism and conservatism, I found higher correlations between self-identification and issue position within the appropriate category. That is, those who thought of liberalism or conservatism as involving social issues showed a significantly higher correlation between their self-placement and their social-issue positions than they did on any other type of issue, and that correlation was higher for them than for those with other types of conceptions. The same was true for those with foreign-policy conceptions and, to a lesser extent, those with economic conceptions of liberalism and conservatism. Those with general conceptions showed moderate correlations across the board.[8] Thus, there may be stronger connections between these symbols and contemporary political issues than earlier studies have indicated.

But these stronger correlations do not fully solve the puzzle. Particularly among the large number of people who give economic definitions to liberalism and conservatism (about one-quarter of the population),[9] the correlations are relatively weak, even for economic issues. And for others who define these words in broad philosophical terms, the definitions are often so general that they raise questions about just what those people mean, especially considering the lack of attention that most people give to political issues. Even if the meanings of these words do reflect understandings of limited issues, a fuller knowledge of how people think of these terms is needed.

A second explanation of the meaning of *liberalism* and *conservatism* has been proposed by Conover and Feldman, who argue that *liberalism* and *conservatism* have largely symbolic meanings and that the terms are not bipolar. That is, a person's ideological identification may largely be a function of the groups and policies that people identify with the concepts of liberalism and conservativism. These identifications are affectively, not cognitively, driven. The power of these symbols derives from their ability to generate strong positive or negative feelings. People like or dislike liberals and/or conservatives because of the groups that they associate with these labels, which have "largely symbolic, nonissue-oriented" meanings.[10] Additionally, the two terms are not part of a single continuum. The symbolic meaning of the label *liberal* is often quite independent of the symbolic meaning attached to the label *conservative*. Conover and Feldman conclude that "the public's usage of ideological labels is more a simplification than a distortion of reality" and that "ideological identifications constitute more a symbolic than issue-oriented link to the political world."[11]

Similarly, Brady and Sniderman suggest that people make sense of these symbols by using a "likability heuristic." Like Conover and Feldman, they posit an affect-driven view of liberalism and conservatism. People know what they like and what they dislike, and they place themselves on issues based on a combination of their liberal-conservative self-placement and their feelings about liberals and conservatives. Unlike Conover and Feldman, however, Brady and Sniderman suggest that it is the relative feelings about liberals and conservatives that is crucial. There may not be bipolarity in the sense that liking liberals leads to disliking conservatives and vice versa, but people do, according to Brady and Sniderman, come to their views on issues by triangulating those views with their feelings about both liberals and conservatives.

These analyses, however, leave a number of unanswered questions. First, linking the meaning of *liberal* and/or *conservative* to people's feelings about secondary groups in the population leaves the question of why people like or dislike those groups and why they associate them with the label *liberal* or *conservative*. Second, and more important, this theory places heavy emphasis on the affective content of these symbols. The use of the terms *liberalism* and *conservativism* reflects how people feel about liberals and conservatives. The problem, though, is that few people have strong feelings about liberals and conservatives. Data from 1980, which Conover and Feldman used in their study, revealed that only about 20 percent of the public gave liberals a rating below 25 or above 75 on the feeling thermometer, and only 24 percent did so for conservatives. Only 8 percent of the population rated liberals or conservatives at the extreme ends of the scale — below 10 or above 90 (see table 2.1).

Table 2.1. Subjects' affective evaluations of liberals and conservatives, 1980

Feeling thermometer score[a]	Subjects (%)	
	Feelings toward liberals	Feelings toward conservatives
0–10	5	1
11–24	4	2
25–44	21	8
45–55	28	26
56–75	32	42
76–89	8	15
90–100	3	6

Note: Data are from the 1980 American National Election Study, by the Center for Political Studies, and were made available through the Interuniversity Consortium for Political and Social Research.

[a]On this scale, zero indicates strong negative feelings; 50, neutral feelings; and 100, strong positive feelings.

People may be driven by their likes and dislikes, but if they are, these likes and dislikes seem to be mild preferences rather than strong feelings. Furthermore, exactly what people like and dislike is not clear. Again, a fuller understanding of the roots of these meanings is required. With these questions in mind, we turn to the interviews.

How people make sense of ideological symbols

I asked people where they saw themselves on a liberal-conservative scale and what the terms *liberal* and *conservative* meant to them. In some cases, the individuals used the terms without any prompting from me when they described some political person or issue. If that was the case, our discussion of these symbols usually followed. If they did not use the terms voluntarily, I raised the issue, usually after we had discussed a series of political issues and figures.

In determining how people used the labels *liberal* and *conservative,* four types of people emerged: those who could not make any sense of these labels, those who saw the labels in terms of policies, those who saw the labels in terms of a particular style of politics, and those who used these labels in terms of both policies and style.

Five people could not use these terms at all: Gail Blair, Laura Rivers, Dave Thomasson, Gus White, and Carla Zeber. They had no understanding of what the terms meant. Laura, a sixty-four-year-old widow with a high school education and a low level of interest in politics, volunteered that information. While discussing the differences between the two parties, she said, "I don't understand *liberal* and *conservative*." I asked her if she had any sense of what the words meant, and she replied, "No. I read it. I read it in the paper. I read the editorials sometimes, and sometimes it's just a little over my head. And I'd like to know more, but then I'll say, 'why bother?' "

The other four people claimed ignorance similar to Laura's when I probed them as to what they thought these terms might mean, and all five of them were unwilling to place themselves on the liberal-conservative scale. None of the five was well educated (Laura was the only one with a high school education), and none had much interest in politics. As we shall see, education seems crucial in determining the type (though not the breadth) of understanding that people bring to these symbols.

The most common type of response to the labels *liberal* and *conservative* was what I call a stylistic response. The individuals saw liberals and conservatives as differing in the way that they approached issues or questions. In a few cases, these styles seemed entirely apolitical, but in most cases the styles were related to certain policy positions. However, in all of the stylistic responses it was clearly the style, not the particular policy position, that was the distinguishing factor.

Two stylistic differences were cited: an orientation-toward-change difference and an open-mindedness difference. The change orientation, as might be expected, is the often-heard difference that liberals will support new ideas and conservatives tend to prefer the status quo. For example, Carol Torrez, an eighty-year-old retired schoolteacher, described why she was a liberal: "Because, you know, I don't want to turn the clock back. I don't want to protect what is just good for me. Senior citizens have got to realize that it's the children that are more important than the senior citizens. Teenagers are more important than the senior citizens if the country is going to survive."

Similarly, George Heath, a fifty-nine-year-old with a strong interest in politics, described why he used to be liberal but was now conservative: " I would say, again with age, when I was a younger man I was for anything. I didn't care what it was. I thought it was good. I thought we were getting too stagnant. Anything. Now I am getting older. I am getting more conservative." When I asked him if he could think of any examples of the things he supported when he was liberal, he said: "Well, anything. I don't know if the Peace Corps is liberal, but I kind of liked the idea. I liked the work program that Roosevelt had there, the CCs [sic] or whatever it was way back. That was good. And now all there is, is programs. What was one? Let me think. I was more for anything new to try, to feel out. Any federal program, I was for. Now I don't know if I would be for any of them."

Sue Doyle, a high-school-educated homemaker, described why she was conservative: "I don't like big drastic changes, whatever it may be. Kind of like, see the situation and so we are going to do this gradually. We can't just up and change everything, because it's very hard for everybody to have total change. It would affect a lot of people's lives. So I am conservative."

Amy Tidrow, a college student, described the liberal-conservative difference this way: "Well, *liberal* just seems like more newer ideas. They are willing to try something different. And *conservative,* it just means a little more like, you know, older ways of doing things, back-to-the-basic-type things."

In a similar fashion, others related liberals to open-mindedness and conservatives to narrowness. For example, Tony Hunter, thirty-eight years old with some college, described the two groups in this way: "The way I look at it, if somebody is described as a liberal, he's an easygoing-type guy. He's very liberal in his attitudes. He's like a laid-back guy. He'll listen to both sides, and he'll take what he feels is the better of the two. There's more space for expansion. And he's not looking down a tunnel. That's the type of guy I think of when somebody says a liberal. I think he's looking at the whole picture." When I asked Tony what he thought *conservative* meant, he said: "Conservative. I think, maybe he's getting tunnel vision a little. Conservative might be looking back on the laurels of what happened in past practices and stuff, and rather than take a chance, let's stay right here—we know this works. Rather than try to expand for the better. I think he's got a little tunnel vision."

John Guidry, a twenty-seven-year-old college graduate, says he is conservative: "Once I get a view into my head, that is my general consensus, that is conservative. You think about it, it's a good cause, and that's that. As opposed to being a little bit liberal and listening to someone else's views. I would look at liberals as someone who will not really stay stable on their views, you know, move either way, to and fro."

Ralph Randolph, twenty-eight years old with a high school education, described conservatives this way: "They are for themselves. I guess they are supposed to be more for themselves. . . . Liberal is more open or more for the people. More listen to the people, to their views and their ideas. . . . I think I would be more liberal. I would be more open and willing to listen to straighten things out."

Ten of the twenty-six interviewees had such stylistic notions of what *liberal* and *conservative* referred to (the other three were Adam Clay, Nancy Gullet, and Martha Nettles). As I mentioned above, some of these stylistic notions were largely apolitical. Three of the people with a change orientation—Adam, Nancy, and Sue—seemed to have no political sense of these words at all. On the other hand, the other seven did have some political sense of what these styles might entail. One example is George's assertion that liberals would support more policies. But these stylistic views of liberal and conservative can lead to "incorrect" policy distinctions. For example, Martha, a fifty-two-year-old secretary with a high school education, cited the bombing of Libya as a liberal action because it showed a willingness to take action. Similarly, Tony, who described liberals and conservatives in terms of open-mindedness and tunnel vision, had this to say about nuclear power:

> In nuclear power, I find myself maybe more liberal. I'm in-
> volved in the power field myself, and I think nuclear power is
> one of the best things that ever came about since the flying
> machine. It's just in its stages, like the flying machine, and it
> has to come through it as such. But I think these people that
> are antinuclear should sit back and look at maybe the Wright
> brothers. There was people that were antiflying then too, but
> look how far we've come in that field. And I think the nu-
> clear field, it can go just as far, and you know, it's working
> for us today. So in that respect, I'm liberal when it comes to
> nuclear. You know it's developing all the time.

Although these policy attributions may be incorrect in terms
of the way we normally characterize contemporary American politics, they are reasonable given these people's visions of what *liberal*
and *conservative* mean. And these are not unreasonable visions.
Certainly a dictionary would support anyone who asserted that the
difference between *liberal* and *conservative* had to do with an
orientation toward change. And research in the area of political
psychology indicates that the closed-minded–open-minded distinction may, in fact, reflect real personality differences between liberals and conservatives.[12] Thus, what a large proportion of people
see as the difference between liberals and conservatives has to do
with two styles of politics. The difference that people see is not
primarily a function of policies that are supported or not supported by liberals and conservatives, or the groups or individuals
who are liberal or conservative. Rather, it is how these people approach political issues themselves. Whether they see themselves as
liberal or conservative, or whether they like liberals or conservatives, is a function of their own orientation toward the relative
importance of a willingness to change or of open-mindedness.
Some of these people liked liberals because of their open-mindedness (such as Tony), while others (such as John) disliked liberals
because they viewed this open-mindedness as wishy-washiness, an
inability to make a decision. Similarly, some people (such as Sue)
preferred "going back to basics," while others (such as Carol) expressed a preference for change and looking to the future.

Eight individuals focused on policies in distinguishing between liberals and conservatives. These eight fell into three categories: those who saw broad, general philosophical policy differences, those who saw social-issue differences, and those who saw economic-issue differences.

Howard Gossage and Al Chambliss, the two people who seemed to conceive of the words *liberal* and *conservative* strictly in terms of economic issues, had the most limited sense of the terms. Howard, sixty-eight years old with three years of high school, simply responded that conservatives "did not overspend" and that, therefore, he was a conservative, but he showed no other use or understanding of the terms. Al, a forty-six-year-old college graduate with a small business, had a fuller sense of the symbols but still seemed to limit them to economic, primarily spending, issues. He said that conservatives want to "spend less and support the work ethic." He described why he thought of himself as conservative: "A balanced budget is important. I don't think we should be allowed to own something without paying. It they want more, they should work more." He also noted that there was one way in which he was liberal, "I see people collect unemployment. They should be supplemented a little more." Still, neither Howard nor Al seemed to use the terms *liberal* and *conservative* except when directly questioned about them.

This was not the case with the three people who saw liberals and conservatives in terms of social issues. Mort Johnson, Walter Beattie, and Clyde Lyle used the words as evaluative tools without prompting. Mort, a sixty-one-year-old government employee with a master's degree, noted that Democrats were liberal because of their stands on "issues such as abortion and school prayer." A liberal himself, he later volunteered that he liked our local congressional representative, Sherwood Boehlart (a moderate-to-liberal Republican): "The conservatives hate his guts, so I like him, because he's doing the things that I think he should be doing." When I asked for an example of that, he mentioned the abortion issue. (Boehlart has been a target of local right-to-life groups who have paid for a billboard advertisement on the highway running through downtown Utica that links Boehlart's stand on abortion to Nazism.)

Similarly, Walter, a fifty-six-year-old white-collar worker with a two-year associate's degree, said that conservative was "more law and order, more religion, back to basics." He, too, evaluated political people by their liberality or conservativeness. For example, he liked Senator Daniel Patrick Moynihan "because he is a liberal."

Finally, from the opposite perspective, Clyde, a twenty-four-year-old college graduate, volunteered almost immediately that he was "a conservative politically." When I asked him what he meant by that, we had the following dialogue:

> Well, I voted for Ronald Reagan both times. I am against abortion. I generally vote Republican unless I know for a fact that the Republican candidate is either extremely liberal or just not a good choice — You know, the Democratic candidate is better.

> *What do you think it means to be a liberal in politics?*

> Well, let's see. Almost anything Mario Cuomo stands for is a liberal idea. And if you look at what he has to say, you can guess right off the bat, that's liberal.

> *Can you give me any examples?*

> Well, for instance, with his stand on abortion. I am personally against it, and I think it is wrong, but I shouldn't foster my moral beliefs on others. Which, if you want to get down to it, that's all laws are anyway — generally held moral beliefs. So to say that you are not going to foster your moral beliefs on anybody, through law, is ridiculous. Because that's what laws are.

Throughout our conversations, all three of these people made it clear that they did evaluate people by whether they were conservative or liberal, but it was also clear that their concept of conservatives and liberals, and what they liked and disliked about the two groups, was a function of their positions on moral and social issues. In fact, their use of the terms, though narrow in scope, was more complete than that of some of the people with broader-issue conceptions, because these three were willing to use the labels to evaluate political figures and parties.[13] However, there was no indication that the symbols of liberal and conservative had anything to do with stands on economic issues or foreign policy. People who have such an association of the terms tend to have fairly strong associations, but the number of such people is limited.[14]

Three people had broad policy conceptions of liberalism and conservatism: Mark Dent, Ted Munson, and Simon Pinella. Mark, a thirty-nine-year-old manual laborer with some college, noted that he was both liberal and conservative, first explaining why he was a liberal: "I think that we have the responsibility for social programs to make sure that everyone has whatever they need. But at the same time I am . . . somewhat conservative as far as that the government shouldn't be running all these things. It shouldn't be involved in all this. So I guess I am not really either thing."

Similarly, Simon, a twenty-five-year-old college graduate, described the difference between conservatives and liberals:

> If they were conservative, it would be maybe against abortion, for more stricter penalties in criminal cases, against more social programs. Conservative may be for big business. Republican, conservatives. More for Moral Majority, rights like that. There's half of it that I would agree with. The other half I'd throw right out the window. Where if someone was a liberal candidate they'd be for more government spending, for more pro-abortion, more for civil rights, which I would be for also. I'd like to be educated more, I guess, as far as civil rights and how they're defined for a lot of people. I guess there's a lot of things I don't agree with when different hiring — equal opportunity practices where people aren't based on qualifications — it's based on your race. It's not the most qualified person, but there are certain quotas companies have to meet. So I guess that's my basic understanding of conservative and liberal.

Aside from answering questions about the meaning of the symbols, neither Simon nor Mark ever used the symbols to evaluate politics in any way. They clearly knew what it meant to be liberal or conservative in broad terms. But the words were not part of their discourse. This was not true of Ted, a thirty-four-year-old white-collar worker with a master's degree. Ted, like the three people with social-issue conceptions, clearly used the words *liberal* and *conservative* in an evaluative sense, volunteering that he liked Democrats because they were the "traditional liberal party":

> What it means to be a liberal is to be concerned about the, quote, social issues. To be very much in favor of equal rights regardless of race, creed, color, religion, sex. It means to me to be very concerned about the amount being spent on the military and how the military spends that money. It means to be concerned on the conservationist side of the environmental issues and in favor of government regulation in people's lives and careers and well-being that helps to make people aware of what the next person is doing. I think we need to care about the fact that there are people that are starving, and that's a legitimate role of government, and I think that's where a liberal stands. And I think we need to be concerned about Dow Chemical dumping sewerage into the Hudson River and to make them clean up their act.

> *What about conservatives?*

> Conservatives are interesting. I don't think there are very many real conservatives left at the national level anyway. I think one of the few that's left is Barry Goldwater, who is disassociating somewhat from the whole operation because he traditionally believed that the proper role of government was to have little if any role in people's day-to-day lives. And he, from what I read, from what he's been saying lately, he perceives the government getting involved the same way the Kennedy-Johnson liberal governments did, only on the opposite end of the spectrum. A true conservative is one who believes let's just have the government be here and maintain the military, maintain what bureaucracy is necessary to run the country, be concerned more with foreign affairs, more than domestic.

Finally, three people had both stylistic and policy conceptions of these symbols. All of them had broad policy linkages with the terms. They identified social and economic issues as being related to being liberal and/or conservative. But they also linked the two symbols to particular styles of politics as well. One of these people, Carl Figueroa, a thirty-five-year-old manual laborer with a high school education, saw the style in terms of a change orientation. But the other two — Ed Stanley, a thirty-three-year-old college graduate and white-collar worker, and Bert Jackson, a forty-year-old health care professional with an advanced degree — saw the stylistic difference as one of idealism versus reality. Both thought that liberals were ideal and abstract in their thinking, whereas conservatives were more pragmatic and realistic. (Both thought of themselves as conservatives.) Ed, for example, thought Democrats were "too liberal, not as thought-out as they should be," and Republicans were "more conservative, more logical, pragmatic." Although all three of these individuals did cite stylistic differences, they also cited other differences. They had a clear understanding of the policies that went with being liberal or conservative. And for Ed and Bert, the style seemed to be a way of indicating the superior reasoning skill of the group that they preferred (conservatives), and the evidence of the superior reasoning was found in the policies each group supported. For example, Bert noted: "Liberal policy is one where we are going to hand out food, and we are going to hand out money to everybody under a certain income. And I sure as hell know this is not going to work. Its intention is to help alleviate a lot of pain and suffering, but that is not what's going to happen, okay? So people get labeled conservative."

There are, then, two very different ways of seeing these symbols. Some people view them as relating to a particular style of politics; others, as relating to particular policy positions.[15] (A few people also seem to see both of these connotations.) Both of these ways of viewing the differences between liberals and conservatives are reasonable. We often define the words in stylistic, especially change-oriented, ways. Political psychology indicates that real stylistic differences do indeed exist between liberals and conservatives.[16] Still, only among those with stylistic definitions did I find any "incorrect" policy attributions. The styles do not always relate to policy positions in obvious ways, and people who make policy attributions on the basis of perceived stylistic differences sometimes "get it wrong."

On the other hand, it is also clear that people with policy attributions sometimes have very narrow views of what those policy differences are. In particular, those with economic definitions seem to have relatively narrow views of what a liberal or a conservative is. This fits in with the low correlations I found between issue position and policy position for those with economic definitions in the 1980 CPS American National Election Study.

In addition, some people use these symbols to make political evaluations, but others do not, and *this is not a function of whether they have a stylistic or a policy orientation toward these symbols* (see table 2.2).

Table 2.2. Relationship between interviewees' conception of ideological symbols and use of symbols as evaluative tools

Use of symbols in evaluation	Conception of ideological symbols		
	Style	Style and policy	Policy
Use	4	2	4
Do not use	6	1	4

Note: Figures are the numbers of interviewees fitting each category. Five people did not have any conception of these symbols and consequently did not use them for evaluation.

Although this is not a representative random national sample, it is clear from the pattern of evaluative use of these terms that either type of conception can lead to political evaluations.[17] Some sense of the symbols is a precondition for using them to sort through politics, but one does not need any kind of policy sense to make such distinctions. Some of the people who like or dislike conservatives and/or liberals and who judge political figures in these terms do so because of the style of politics they associate with these groups, not because of the policy positions these groups take. (Others, of course, like or dislike them because of the policy positions they take.) These findings are in line with those of Conover and Feldman, and Brady and Sniderman. The non-policy-oriented affective attachment to liberals and conservatives that Conover and Feldman found, and Brady and Sniderman's "likability heuristic" (the use of a like or dislike of these groups to make judgments), may be explained by stylistic conceptions of these symbols. Therefore, we need to be careful in drawing conclusions about the liberalness or conservativeness of the public. To some, these are policy conceptions (either broad or narrow), but to others they represent a way to relate to the political world. Furthermore, although these symbols were used as evaluative tools by about half of the people who had a sense of their meaning, they were not particularly important symbols in that regard. For most people, they were useful but were only tangential to the way in which those people constructed their political views. In only four cases did these symbols take on a relatively central place in the way these people thought about politics. (Note that one of these people (Tony) had a stylistic conception of these symbols, two of them (Clyde and Walter) had social policy conceptions, and the other (Carl) had both broad policy and stylistic conceptions.) Thus, although the way these symbols are conceptualized tells us something about how people see politics, the symbols themselves are rarely central to people's views of the political world. The symbols seem, instead, to serve more as signposts that help people maneuver through the world of politics, and the meaning of those signposts can differ greatly, depending upon whether the people have a stylistic or a policy conception. I will return shortly to this difference between stylistic and policy views of politics to discuss why these differences arise and their implications, but first we need to look at how people conceive of the political parties.

Partisan symbols

As was noted above, partisanship is another factor that may help individuals sort through the complexity of politics and come to opinions about issues and candidates. Most people can be placed on the party identification scale, and people's attachments to parties may make it easy for them to decide what and who they like or dislike. As with ideological symbols, however, knowing who people like or dislike leaves the question of why they like or dislike these groups. Why do people prefer Democrats or Republicans?

In addition, as Wattenberg has shown, there has been a marked decline in people's images of the parties. More than a third of the population has no image at all of the parties; they cannot name one thing that they like or dislike about either party. I have found that people with no substantive image of the parties show no consistent differences in issue positions even when they claim to identify with one of the parties.[18] Thus, it may be that parties no longer serve as the kind of cue they once did. The changing nature of politics in our candidate-centered, media age may have rendered the parties impotent as a structuring force in how people think about the political world. Kinder and Sears note that "Democrats and Republicans in the general public are difficult to distinguish,"[19] and it may be that this makes it difficult for people to use party affiliation as a way of sorting through politics.

Two previous studies looked briefly at this issue of what parties and party attachments mean to people. In *Party Image and Electoral Behavior*, Trilling traced the meaning of party from 1952 to 1972.[20] He classified people as to whether they see parties in terms of people in the party, managers of government, broad philosophy, or domestic or foreign policies. He found that "short term political issues" had only a limited effect on the images that people held. This, he argued, reflected "the failure of political parties to polarize the electorate around these issues."[21] Thus, issues such as race or Vietnam may have a short-term impact on the images of parties, but they have not penetrated more deeply.[22]

Wattenberg, in *The Decline of American Political Parties, 1952–1984*, discussed changes in party images. He concluded, as was noted above, that the major change was a decline in any kind of image for either party: "In sum, neither party now has a very firmly entrenched positive or negative public image on such issues [as economic/welfare policy] compared to two decades ago."[23]

Still, neither of these two studies delves deeply into how people relate to the parties. We need to take a closer look at how people make sense of the political parties.

How people make sense of partisan symbols

The most striking thing about people's visions of the political parties is how unimportant the parties actually are in helping people think about politics. In fact, nine of my twenty-six interviewees could not cite any difference at all between the parties or anything they liked or disliked about either party; one other person saw no differences but expressed dislike for both parties. Thus, for 38 percent of these people, party made no difference. For example, when I asked Adam Clay what the differences were between the parties, he said:

> None. Just who is in at the time. It seems to change from year to year, four years to four years. Presidents, what the party believes and stands for.

> *So you don't think there are any differences?*

> Not really. I don't think it's a strict line. Republicans do this, and Democrats do this. It's just a general, I suppose, who you like at the time when you go and vote one way or the other.

Later, he said: "You hear that so-and-so used to be a liberal and is now a conservative, and someone was a Democrat and switched to a Republican, and now is a Right-to-Life party or whatever. People change so drastically that you can't place a label on them. I think it's hard to place labels on people because people change. It's hard to place a label on someone who changes."

Similarly, Ralph Randolph said: "I don't really see all that much difference. I mean I think they are basically the same as far as I know about them." And Laura Rivers said: "Is there really [a difference] other than one's a donkey and one's an elephant? Really, I mean their thoughts have to be geared to the American people. . . . I really don't think so."

For these ten people, then, there was no difference between the parties, and party affiliation did not help them decide which side of an issue to be on or what to think about a particular policy. As was noted above, nine of them could say nothing positive or negative about either party. The one exception was Bert Jackson, who did not like either party (nor very much else about politics):

> You see a lot of people swapping parties. You see people who used to be Republicans that are now independents, and Dem-

ocrats that are now this. What is a Democrat, and what is a
Republican? I think that what's happened is that we have a
blur. I don't think the two of them are distinct anymore.
There is not a black and a white anymore. I think everything
sort of is like blending, being various shades of gray. We still
have some black, and we still have some white, but there is a
lot of gray in there. Of course, for the purpose of elections
and for the purpose of party funding and party backing, they
take on a name, but I don't really believe that label. . . . As
soon as that guy gets in office, he ends up being a blowhard,
and he is just emitting hot air. Then he's worthless also, even
to his party.

For eight of these ten, including Adam, Ralph, and Bert,
party is not of any use in making political evaluations and judgments. (The others were Howard Gossage, John Guidry, Nancy
Gullet, Gus White, and Carla Zeber.) However, Laura Rivers and
Dave Thomasson expressed some loyalty to the Democrats when it
came to voting, in spite of seeing no difference between the parties.
Their loyalty sprang from a historical allegiance to the party dating
back to the days of Franklin Roosevelt and Harry Truman. As
Dave put it:

Well, this may amaze you. When I went in to register, I had a
coin I flipped in the air. I was going whichever way — heads
would be a Republican, tails would be a Democrat. And so it
came up tails. And this happened at the time that Al Smith
was running for president. Of course, he was defeated quite
soundly by Herbert Hoover. And then Hoover's four years
were detrimental because of the stock market crash. So that
gave me reason to stick close with the Democrats. Franklin
Roosevelt, he started a lot of these programs that helped my
kind. CCC for the youth. You got $30 a month — $5 for
spending money, $25 went to your family — which was a good
idea and it kept you off the streets and stuff like that. There
was NRA, all kinds of programs. And that's why he defeated
Landon so solidly in 1936.

The loyalty that they felt made a difference in the voting

booth, unless some other force superseded, but aside from that, party was not important in structuring their thoughts about politics. They never mentioned party unless specifically asked about it, but they still felt they should vote for Democrats because of what Democrats had done in the 1930s.

Except for Laura and Dave, these ten people made no use of partisanship when they thought about politics. Even for Laura and Dave, partisanship played only the smallest role in helping them make sense of politics.

For the other sixteen people that I talked to, however, party had some meaning. They saw some differences between the parties, and those differences helped most of them sort through politics. As with ideological symbols, a distinction can be drawn between those with stylistic conceptions and those with policy conceptions. Some people see party as a function of the issue positions that the parties take, while others see party as representing distinct styles of politics, and still others see both distinctions as being relevant.

Five of these people saw the parties as representing different styles of politics. For example, Amy Tidrow described the difference this way:

[The Republicans] stick up for themselves. Ronald Reagan, he sticks up for himself, and he really says what he wants. Well, sometimes he says what he wants to say, but he knows what he wants to say. And his policies—he makes one and he just goes through with it no matter what. He stays with one thing. And I guess I would rather be a Republican. I think I am more Republican, because the more I think about it, Democratic is kind of, you pick a policy and you go through with it, but along the way maybe you will alter it a little bit. You know, you are more open-minded in a way, I guess. And fairer. Maybe it's just, you really don't know what you want to do.

Carol Torrez said she thought the difference was that Democrats were more understanding than Republicans. Gail Blair and Martha Nettles both thought the difference was a class difference. As Gail put it, "Democrats were poor. The Republicans were rich." Martha said Democrats came from the lower class, the Republicans from the upper class. It was clear in that Gail and Martha did not mean that Democratic policies supported the poor and Republican policies supported the rich. In fact, they both thought that party made no difference in terms of policy outcomes. To them, party differences were simply a function of the different kinds of people that were found in the two parties.

Tony Hunter told me that what distinguishes between the parties is a sense of loyalty: "Some people are staunch Republicans and staunch Democrats and think in those lines." But he did not think party made much difference. Others might be loyal to their party, and they might even think there were policy differences, but he did not see party as important.

For Tony and Martha, these style differences have no impact. They do not use party in any way when it comes to evaluating candidates or issues. Tony is a registered Democrat so that he can vote in the primaries, but party clearly has no substantive effect on how he judges candidates. (He says he registered as a Democrat "because my parents were Democrats.")

On the other hand, Gail, Carol, and Amy do use stylistic differences to help them evaluate political figures. They see no real policy differences between the parties, but knowing that certain kinds of people are Democrats or Republicans is helpful to them at election time. Still, their use of party is a minor factor in helping them sort out politics. They each voted for and supported people in both parties at various times, and their thoughts about politics were only slightly influenced by their views on partisanship.

Five other interviewees distinguished between the parties solely by policy differences. Mort Johnson and Clyde Lyle saw these differences largely in terms of the same social-policy differences they cited when discussing ideological symbols. Mort, for example, said:

I think the Democrats are probably more liberal than the Republicans, and I tend to side more with their views than with the Republican views.

So when you say the Democrats tend to be more liberal, what views in particular make them more liberal?

I think issues such as abortion, school prayer, da-di-da-di-da. Things like that, to my way of thinking, are conservative views. Freedom of choice and there-is-no-need-for-school-prayer would be more liberal.

Sue Doyle and Simon Pinella cited economic and government-spending policy differences. Sue, for example, explained why she supported Republicans: "Well, the Democrats are very socialistic, and they try to, I think, give too much away. . . . The Democrats seem to be a lot of giveaways, and they're the ones that are into constantly adding on social programs or whatever. Where the Republicans are trying to do the opposite. Only keep what's needed."

Walter Beattie cited both social and economic policy, noting that spending, law and order, defense, and religion were areas in which the two parties differed.

For these five people, party was of some use in thinking about politics. For Sue, the use of party was minimal. She seemed to think about things in partisan terms only occasionally. For the other four, however, partisanship played a moderate role in helping them sort out politics. Clyde and Simon generally supported Republicans, while Mort and Walter preferred Democrats. These four used party to help keep track of who they liked and disliked.

In all of these cases, issues were more important than party, and all of these people said that they would support a member of the other party who had the right policy positions. For example, when I asked Clyde why he tended to support the Republican party, he said:

For the most part, Republicans tend to be more conservative, and Democrats tend to be more liberal, but that isn't always the case. On a national level it tends to be more so than on a local level.

And when you vote, you tend to vote for . . .

Conservative Republicans and Democrats.

These five people might use party as a shorthand to help them decide who they would support, but party was clearly a surrogate for particular policy positions. Party, by itself, was not central to their thinking. Rather, party related to some issues or policies that they saw as crucial.

The remaining six people I talked with noted both policy and style distinctions between the parties. Carl Figueroa, for example, described the differences between the parties:

> The Democrats take a primarily liberal line. The Republicans take a conservative line. Democrats are primarily for the poor. Republicans more or less lean toward the rich. Democrats, they just seem to weaken the country. I think the Republicans are more for the patriotism. The Democrats are more for women's rights, I guess, whereby the Republicans are more for—I'm not saying they're against women's rights, but they're for limiting it. They don't want things to go completely out of control, as far as ERA and all that stuff is concerned. Primarily I think the Democrats are mostly liberal. The Republicans are conservatives. Right-wing and left-wing, you know, however you want to differentiate.

When I asked him what he meant by *liberal* and *conservative,* he said: "Liberals I tie in more or less with chaos. Things like this. They want change." Thus, there is a difference in policy, but there is also a difference in style. The Democrats are chaotic. The Republicans are less rash.

Ed Stanley said the differences between the parties were, first of all, differences in economic policy, and second, "I guess I look upon the Democrats as being abstract thinkers and the Republicans as being quantitative thinkers." Al Chambliss preferred Republicans because "they are less likely to have more welfare programs and other programs." His preference was also affected by his view of Democrats: "[they] are always so afraid of making changes. They want to get reelected. . . . They have no leadership."

For these six (the other three were Mark Dent, George Heath, and Ted Munson), policy differences combine with differences in style. That made the parties potentially even more important than they were for those who saw only one of these types of differences. In one case, that was clearly true: For Carl, party was absolutely central. He related most issues to partisan positions, and he clearly liked all that was Republican and disliked all that was Democratic. He did not know the party positions on some policies, and in those cases he sometimes supported the "Democratic" side, but I have no doubt, after talking to him, that he would seriously reconsider that position if it was clear to him that Republicans were on the other side of the issue. In fact, the one time that he had supported a Democrat was, in his mind, a disaster. He noted that he had been drawn to Jimmy Carter in 1976, "But I am . . . disillusioned because I campaigned for Carter, gave Carter the chance and stuff, the benefit of the doubt, and I went against a Republican for a Democrat and got burnt real badly, and I'm very leery about that." His single experience in switching parties reinforced his views about the importance of sticking with the Republicans.

For another three of these six people, party played a moderately strong role in how they made sense of politics. Like most of the people with policy orientations toward the parties, Al, Ed, and Ted saw party was an aid in understanding politics. Al and Ed were Republicans, and Ted was a Democrat. They tended to support the political leaders and policy positions of their parties. However, like the policy-oriented people, they too were willing to desert their party on occasions when they did not think the party was living up to their vision of it. Even so, because that vision was more than simply the policy position of the party, they were more stable in their party support than people with only policy orientations.

For one of these individuals with both a stylistic and a policy orientation toward the parties, party played only a minor role. George recognized differences between the parties but was clearly willing to support the policies or leaders of either party. He did not feel a strong attachment to either party. In fact, he thought the most important reason to support one of the parties (in his case, the Democrats) was that "if you ever did need them, which thank God I never needed the party, you could always say, 'hey, I've been a Democrat for so many years.' " The local party might be able to help you, but only if you were a supporter. George said that if he did not know anything about either candidate, he would vote the party line, but given his interest in politics, that would rarely be the case. For George, the differences between the parties were not that important. Party was of little use in sorting out politics.

Mark Dent did not use party at all as a guide in thinking about politics. He cited differences between the parties, noting that "Republicans spend money on the military, and the Democrats spend it on social issues," that Democrats "try to appeal to everybody [and are] wishy-washy," and that Republicans "are more oriented to the special interests." But these differences did not matter much to Mark. He did not like either party. He thought they both spent too much money, even if they spent it on different things. Mark voted for Walter Mondale in 1984 because he did not want Ronald Reagan to win too large a landslide, and in 1976 he voted for the Libertarian candidate for president. The Democratic and Republican parties are not a part of the way Mark thinks about politics.

As with ideological symbols, people tend to use party in different ways when they try to understand politics. For some, party represents distinctive policy positions, but for others, party represents different styles. But party is rarely central in people's views of politics. Party can, and does, help some people make sense of the issues and figures that appear on the political scene. As table 2.3 shows, only a little more than half of the people I talked to used party at all in an evaluative sense, and only one had a way of sorting out politics with party at the center. In seven other cases, party played a moderately useful role in helping people understand politics, and in another seven, party played a small role.

Table 2.3. Relationship between interviewees' conception of party symbols and use of symbols as evaluative tools

Level of use of symbols in evaluation	Conception of party symbols			
	None	Style	Style and policy	Policy
High	0	0	1	0
Moderate	0	0	3	4
Low	2	3	1	1
None	8	2	1	0

Note: Figures are the numbers of interviewees fitting each category.

One other point is striking when considering the ideas that people have about the parties, and that is how many of them have a sense of history with regard to the parties. Although I never asked a question about previous party affiliation or the party affiliation of the parents of these individuals, half of them raised at least one of these issues. (Once they raised them, of course, we often went on to discuss them in greater length, but I never initiated these topics.) People have a sense of the development of parties and of some of the changes that have occurred. Nine of them mentioned that they first developed an allegiance to one of the parties because of the allegiance of their parents, and seven of them talked about changing allegiance to one or the other of the parties because of changes in either their own views or changes in the parties. This contrasts strongly with the use of ideologicial symbols; only one individual, Walter, mentioned these symbols in terms of family background, noting that he was raised in a "Democratic liberal" household. Thus, people can and do develop a sense of loyalty to the parties that may run deeper than their attachment to ideological symbols. Laura and Dave have such an attachment, for example. But these historically based attachments do not seem very strong, nor do they seem to be of more than minor use in helping to make sense of politics.

Stylistic and policy conceptions of politics

The most important point to emerge from this look at the use of ideological and party symbols is that some people relate these symbols to policy differences and some relate them to different styles of politics (and others see both differences). These conceptions indicate very different approaches to sorting through the political arena. Furthermore, the style and policy orientations seem to be consistent for both ideological and party symbols.

As table 2.4 indicates, only one individual (Sue Doyle) had a

Table 2.4. Relationship between interviewees' conception of party symbols and conception of ideological symbols

Conception of ideological symbols	Conception of party symbols			
	None	Style	Style and policy	Policy
None	4	1	0	0
Style	4	4	1	1
Style and policy	1	0	2	0
Policy	1	0	3	4

Note: Figures are the numbers of interviewees fitting each category.

straight policy orientation toward one of these identifications (party) and a straight stylistic orientation toward the other (ideology). Some of those with a single orientation toward one identification exhibited both identifications toward the other, but a majority had the same orientation toward both types of symbols.

If style is more important to some than policy, then we should not be surprised if many of these people support political leaders whose policies they say they do not like. In the end, they may be more impressed with or more concerned about whether they think those candidates are the right kind of leader (Do they act rashly or not? Do they exercise proper degrees of leadership?) than whether they agree with the candidates on unemployment or abortion or military spending. Others, however, are more likely to relate to politics in terms of particular policy areas. Some will have a narrow view, others a broader one, but here the operative question is, What policies do the political leaders support?

These differences in the way people are oriented toward these symbols illustrate differing approaches to political evaluation. We will explore these differences more fully in Chapter 8, when we look at the broader patterns of political thinking that people have and how people evaluate our political leaders. As we will see, most people develop a mix of these two very different ways of understanding politics as they interpret and judge political events and figures, but within that mix, they also tend to rely more heavily on one of these two modes of thinking.

Stylistic orientations toward politics are not simply a function of image and the media. Rather, style seems to be one method that people use to judge future performance. In a world filled with uncertainty, some people use the styles that they judge to be effective in dealing with the world as important guides in evaluating political leaders. Too, people often find it easier to understand style than the complications of policy, particularly in our media-filled environment. People can see from their own life experiences what types of ways of dealing with problems — what approaches or styles — seem to be the most or least effective. We will explore more evidence for these assertions later (particularly in Chapters 6 and 7), but for now it is important to recognize the differences in orientations and the role that they play in helping people make sense of politics.

Finally, there is the question of why people have these different orientations toward these symbols or toward politics in general. It is difficult in a sample of only twenty-six people to make generalizations, but two factors do stand out: education and political interest.

As table 2.5 indicates, greater education seems to lead to policy notions of ideological symbols, as does greater interest in politics. Those with less education and less interest are more likely to think in stylistic terms.

Table 2.5. Relationship between interviewees' conception of ideological symbols and interviewees' education and interest in politics

Level of education or interest in politics	Conception of ideological symbols			
	None	Style	Style and policy	Policy
Education				
Grade school	2	1	0	0
Some high school	2	0	0	1
High school	1	3	1	0
Some college	0	4	0	2
College	0	2	1	3
Advanced degree	0	0	1	2
Interest in politics				
Low	3	3	0	1
Moderate	2	6	1	4
High	0	1	2	3

Note: Figures are the numbers of interviewees fitting each category.

Similarly, as table 2.6 indicates, those without a high school degree do not have a clear image of the parties. Only one of the six people with minimal education had any type of image (Gail, who had a stylistic image). On the other hand, those with greater education were spread fairly evenly across the different types of orientation. In addition, all of those individuals with high interest in politics saw policy distinctions between the parties, though some mixed those distinctions with stylistic distinctions, and five of the seven individuals with a low interest in politics saw no difference between the parties.

Both education and political interest, then, seem to lead to familiarity with the policy differences between the parties and between liberals and conservatives, and lack of education and a lim-

Table 2.6. Relationship between interviewees' conception of party symbols and interviewees' education and interest in politics

Level of education or interest in politics	Conception of party symbols			
	None	Style	Style and policy	Policy
Education				
Grade school	3	0	0	0
Some high school	2	1	0	0
High school	2	1	1	1
Some college	1	2	2	1
College	1	1	2	2
Advanced degree	1	0	1	1
Interest in politics				
Low	5	0	0	2
Moderate	5	5	2	1
High	0	0	4	2

Note: Figures are the numbers of interviewees fitting each category.

ited interest in politics seem to lead to a view of politics in terms of how people act as opposed to what they do. For people with limited education and interest, it may in fact be easier to make decisions based upon whether they think a person acts properly (or in ways likely to lead to good outcomes) rather than to try to evaluate the propriety of a particular policy.

Some of this education and interest difference reflects familiarity with the language of politics. As we will see, particularly for those with both style and policy orientations toward one or both of these symbols, some people who can cite policy distinctions still rely on stylistic notions to make political judgments. On the other hand, knowing or recognizing policy distinctions gives an individual more information that can be useful in trying to make sense of politics.

Conclusions

Partisanship and ideology seem to serve as signposts on the road map of politics. Many people, though clearly not all, use these signposts to steer through the maze of political events and figures that confront them. For some the signposts represent policy positions, for some they represent differing styles of politics, and for some they represent both of these things.

But these symbols are just signposts. They do not, except in rare circumstances, represent the map itself. They are not central organizing concepts for most people attempting to maneuver through the political world. Of the twenty-six people I talked with, party was a central idea for only one (Carl), and for him and three others (Tony, Walter, and Clyde) ideological symbols played a central role. These symbols sometimes help people decide who to vote for or whether they like a particular political figure.

The results found here also help explain the results found by other researchers such as Conover and Feldman, and Brady and Sniderman, who posit affective attachments to political symbols without any explanation of the causes of those attachments. For many, that attachment is based on a notion of which styles of politics are likely to succeed or fail.

After talking at length with these individuals, it is impossible to conclude that party identification or ideological identification is an important source of the political ideas that people hold. These identifications serve as guides to the world of politics, but if we want to know how people make sense of that world, we need to look in other places.

It is also clear that people's conceptions of party and ideological symbols do not indicate a very sophisticated sense of politics. Stylistic conceptions create a simplistic way of judging politics. People and policies are judged on whether they meet stylistic criteria (liberals are too wishy-washy, or conservatives are too closed-minded), not by any clear sense of what the political and social consequences of some policy or change in leadership might be (though, as we shall see, style is not divorced from consequences). Most of the policy conceptions that I found were relatively narrow. As Luskin has noted in his exhaustive review of attempts to measure political sophistication, the mass public does not have a sophisticated sense of politics. But as he and others such as Kinder[24] also note, this leaves unanswered the question of exactly how people do make sense of politics. The style-policy distinction developed here can begin to answer that question, but only by understanding the kinds of ideas that are central to people's thoughts can we begin to understand the dynamics of public opinion. It is to those central ideas that we now turn.

3

The centrality of trust

Perhaps the most striking thing about my talks with these twenty-six individuals was the importance of trust in how people thought about the political world. In seventeen of the twenty-six interviews some aspect of trust came up in responses to the first question I asked, which was always a question about their interest in politics. Attitudes toward trust underlie and connect many of the opinions that people hold. Trust—whether people have faith in their leaders and/or other people—is a crucial part of how people think about politics.

This does not mean that the level of trust is the determining factor that structures the attitudes people have. Rather, it is a central focus that shapes the way people think about the world. Trust is but one of these shaping factors. In this chapter we will explore how attitudes toward trust shape people's views of politics. We will leave the interaction of trust with other shaping attitudes for later.

Patterns of trust

Two independent attitudes fall under the category of trust: attitudes toward the system and attitudes toward other people, particularly political leaders. Political scientists have debated

whether the steep decline in trust found in survey questions in the
1960s and 1970s reflected a decline in trust in the system or dissatisfaction with leaders.[1] My discussions with people indicate that
these attitudes are independent of each other. People can trust the
system but not other people, or they can trust other people but not
the system. These attitudes intersect to create four distinct patterns, or categories, of trust (see table 3.1). However, there is much
variation within each category. People differ in the extent to which
they trust. Some trust everyone, and some trust nobody, but most
are somewhere in between. Sometimes they trust people, and sometimes they do not. Within each category, therefore, is a continuum,
with some people approaching the ideal type, and others falling
less clearly within the category. It was possible to distinguish the
basic tendencies in terms of trust present in each individual, however, and that is what these categories represent.

Table 3.1. Patterns of trust

Belief about system	Attitude toward individuals	
	Trust	Distrust
Honest	Supporters	"democrats"
Corrupt	Skeptics	Cynics

   The first category is the supporters. These people trust both
the system and our leaders as individuals. They believe the system
works, and they have faith in the motives of those in office. They
differ in the extent to which they focus on the system or people as
the reason for their trust, but their basic attitude is one of support.
Seven of the twenty-six interviewees fell into this category.
   Second, we have the skeptics. Like the supporters, they have
faith in our leaders as individuals. They believe that people are
basically honest. However, they think that the system corrupts people. Money, power, and the need for political favors are among the
factors within the system that they see as corrupting people. They
believe that the good intentions of those in power will often be
thwarted by a corrupt political system. This category had the most
respondents — nine individuals.
   Next are the cynics. Like the skeptics, they believe the system
is corrupting, but their distrust goes further. They do not believe

that good people are led astray by the system. Rather, they believe that the people in the system are corrupt and dishonest to begin with. Some people in this category restrict their cynicism to people in politics, believing that anyone who gets involved (or almost anyone who gets involved) is corrupt to begin with, but others outside the political realm may be honest. Other cynics believe that corruption is part of human nature, that all people are, by nature, at least partially bad and should not be trusted. At this level, cynicism runs very deep. Seven people fell into the cynics category.

Finally, there are the "democrats." Only three individuals fit in this category. These people do not trust our leaders. However, they believe that the system can keep our leaders honest, at least some of the time. Because they do not have faith in people, their belief in the ability of the system to ferret out corruption is low, but they do believe that the system is our one hope. If not for the system, all would be lost. It is the democratic nature of the system—the vote and its consequences—that they see as restraining corruption. Hence, I have labeled them democrats.

Let us look more closely at each of these patterns and the consequences that they have for how people think about politics.

THE SKEPTICS

The most common pattern of trust was what I have labeled skeptics. People in this category had a basic distrust of the political system but did not think that our leaders were necessarily bad. The nine people who fell into this category were Walter Beattie, Al Chambliss, Sue Doyle, Mort Johnson, Clyde Lyle, Ted Munson, Amy Tidrow, Carol Torrez, and Carla Zeber. Probably the purest and best-developed example of someone with this pattern was Sue. When I asked her why she was not very interested in politics, she responded:

> My feeling in politics—I can't say everybody is crooked, but there is a lot of people going into it that are honest and want to do a good job, but when they get in and see the system, they'll see what goes on. You do me a favor, and I do you a favor, and now you owe me, and blah-blah-blah. A lot of times they aren't able to do what they set out to do because of what goes on in politics, the owing and the whatever. And

sometimes they have to do things that they don't want to do, but, say, they want one thing for their area. Then they are going to have to vote for ten other things that they really don't think is right or whatever so they can get what they want for their area. And there's a lot of corruption, and you can't always believe what they say. I'm a realist in that department. And I believe a lot of people go in with good intentions, and there are a lot of good people. And it's just a topic that I don't waste a lot of time with because I don't feel as though I can do too much about it. I can vote, which I do. But I don't get into it that much.

In this category, the system is what causes the corruption, and this led Sue to low involvement in politics. In her case, as well, lack of trust in the system was part of a more complex vision of how society should operate. In Sue's worldview, what was natural was good, and anything that interfered with the natural was interfering with what should be. Government was one such thing. It corrupted people and hindered the functioning of society. Talking about unemployment, Sue said:

Well, I feel as though there are jobs out there. And there's not going to be jobs for everybody. Realistically, this is the world here, and the nature or whatever. I feel the strong survive. And that's the way it is out in the woods with the animals and the birds. And for some reason today, maybe because of what's been going on and the way people have been thinking lately, somebody wants to have a lot of money and high positions and whatever, but they're not capable. They don't have it, whether it be physically maybe or their capabilities in education, their ability to learn. Maybe they don't have it, to be this big executive and to make a lot of money and whatever.

Thus, for Sue, government corrupted in part because it interfered with what was natural. It forced people to make deals they would not otherwise make. It led to favors and dishonesty. Sue preferred foods without any additives, opposed mothers working rather than staying home with their children, and had no faith in politics—all because she opposed the distortion of what was natural. To Sue, the most corrupting influence of all was money: "Money talks. Your big industries and anybody with money can go lobby. And they can give people—congressmen and senators— money and support. Basically they can get what they want. That's the way it is."

Sue's complete ideology was not common to the others in this category, but the distrust of money was, especially the role of money in campaigns. As Ted put it:

> They certainly have to get the money from somewhere, and they have to feel obligated to the people that gave them the money.

> *And if you could eliminate that problem, do you think they would probably do a much better job?*

> I think that they would be more responsive. They would go back to voting their consciences instead of voting whoever gave them the money last about an issue.

> *So politics doesn't attract intrinsically corrupt people?*

> No, I think the system causes them to, and I don't even want to call it corrupt because it's not like they're taking bribes. I think it's just the way it is. If a congressman gets a thousand-dollar donation from the dairy farmers' cooperative in favor of only black and white cows, when that comes up for a vote saying we're going to ban all brown cows, and all cows are only going to be black and white, he's got little choice but to vote on the side of the issue that those people gave him the money for. He's almost got an ethical obligation to do it. Otherwise he shouldn't have taken the money. If he turns down the money from too many people, then he doesn't get elected.

The people in this group differed, of course, in the extent to which they saw such corruption as present. Sue was at one extreme, having very little faith that honest people could do anything about the corruption that existed. Also at that end of the scale was Clyde. When I asked him if we could trust our political leaders, he replied:

Some, yes. A lot, no.

Why not?

I get the impression that a lot of times the easiest way to sometimes win an election is to be a little dishonest about it — either what your opponent stands for, or what you stand for, your credentials or your opponents credentials.

So you think it has something to do with the system then, or does it have to do with them as individuals?

Well, the system in part, yes. And the type of individuals that are mostly attracted to a political career I don't think are the type to be scrupulously honest about things.

Clyde came very close here to expressing the attitude found among the cynics, that all individuals in the system, as well as the system itself, were corrupt. What kept him in the skeptical category was his insistence that some leaders were honest. Still, he was among the most skeptical of the skeptics.

At the other end of the scale are Amy, Walter, and Carol who were less skeptical that good individuals could overcome the corruption of the system. In Amy's case, the corruption came not so much from money and influence as from the environment in which political leaders lived. Amy explained why we couldn't trust our leaders:

They earn a lot of money, and I think that after a while it is not their fault, but they are just removed from everyday life. They have lunches all the time and they have all the higher-type thing than the normal everyday person would be involved in. And I think that it's not really their fault, but they get to the point where they really don't know what the people want. They just think, "Well, this is what sounds good, so this is what the people want." They don't really go out and get information from the people they are supposed to represent. They just try to make it sound like, "Well, I am for the good of the people, and I am doing this and I am doing that." And even if it is not what the people want, they make it sound like it is to themselves.

Walter thought that most of our leaders had our best interest at heart, but they often got sidetracked by the demands of the job, so that they traded votes at the expense of the nation. Carol found the influence of money to be troublesome but had not given up hope that good leaders would surface. She believed that a little reform could help solve this problem:

> [Politicians] are caught. They have to have such big sums today to get reelected. They have to depend on big givers to a great extent. So I think one of the big things is to cut out all of those contributions. . . . We need more men with independent views. There have been so many fine ones and so many who mean well. . . . It's a very difficult situation that our congressmen are in.

The other skeptics — Al, Mort, Ted, and Carla — fell in between the pessimism (bordering on cynicism) of Sue and Clyde, and the relative optimism of Amy, Walter, and Carol. The skeptics, then, often believed that reforming the system could help. If you changed the system, you might allow the honest politicians and leaders to do their jobs. Campaign finance reform was a popular topic among these people, with six of them raising the issue (I never asked anyone if they supported campaign finance unless they first brought up the subject). But their most common suggestion for reform was more activity by the public. Honest individuals were needed to keep an eye on the system. As Al noted: "I think [the public] feels that politicians are basically corrupt. They feel it's useless, it's fruitless [to get involved]. I think people in general are not bold enough."

All of the skeptics, including Sue, thought that having more people vote would improve the situation (though Sue was quite skeptical of how much improvement it would bring). Most of the skeptics were quite sure that more involvement by people would help a great deal. Thus, this set of attitudes leads people toward supporting reform of the system and advocating political activity by the public (with the exception of the most pessimistic of the skeptical, who are less sanguine about the possibilities of political action).

There is another result of this pattern of attitudes. When voting, all of these individuals thought that the character of the candidate was important. Since we had a rotten system that was often corrupting, it was essential to find political leaders who were honest and trustworthy. One of the questions I asked everyone was what kinds of things were important in deciding who to vote for in a presidential election. Six of these nine individuals talked primarily about personal quality and character. Ted, for example, stated what was most important to him: "They need to gain the trust of the people and make themselves believable to the people if they are going to be president. If they're going to be in Congress, they need to be people of ethics and honor and conscience." Walter said: "You vote for who you think is the better person," making it clear that being a better person was a function of character, not policy positions.

Only one of these people, Mort, cited policy reasons as his primary consideration, saying that he looked to see "if he thinks the way I do." When I asked him what he meant by that, he replied: "Primarily on the issues."

Two others, Sue and Clyde, cited a combination of issue positions and character. They too believed that honesty was essential, but they tempered that view with a consideration of the issues as well.

Two of the three skeptics who cited issues as being important, Sue and Clyde, were the most pessimistic skeptics. They had the least faith in the ability of good people to overcome the corrupting influences of the system, though they did have more faith in this than the cynics. As we shall see, the cynics, if they had any thought at all on the issue, were also likely to cite policy positions as being more important than character.

Skepticism, then, leads to a reformist bent. It generally leads to a support of political activity by individuals and to an emphasis on character in making voting decisions. We will return to the impact of these different patterns of thought at the end of the chapter. But now we need to turn to the other three groups.

THE CYNICS

The seven people who fell into the cynical category—Gail Blair, Mark Dent, Carl Figueroa, Howard Gossage, Bert Jackson, Dave Thomasson, and Gus White—shared a lack of faith in both the political system and our political leaders. Like the skeptics, they saw the system, particularly the influence of money, as corrupting. As Carl put it:

> Once you become politically inclined, it's money, the dollar sign, the almighty dollar. You're making loads of bucks. You're up there in the upper class. I mean, to get there in the first place you have to have bucks to campaign, do all that. You're going to be rich and of course you're thinking in terms of yourself. Like I said, that's the problem. There's a lot of people who are just thinking in terms of themselves, especially in the political arena. They take care of themselves. They don't care. You know, they say, what is it about absolute power corrupts or something like this? I mean, once you got money, you think you reach a point where you have enough, but you never do. You always get greedy and need more and more. And that's the same thing with the politicians, the rich. They want more and more. There is always that drive to make more, to get more.

For these seven, the pessimism ran deeper than it did for the skeptics. Not only did money and/or power corrupt (none of the cynics thought corruption was due to factors such as vote trading or not listening to the people, as some of the skeptics did), but also nothing could be done about it. As Mark said, in discussing the tax system:

> Like everything else, it's set up to help the people who set it up. The average man pays much more than his share. I mean, I hear all the time the statistics on it. The biggest corporations pay nothing. I can't reel off any numbers on that, but the average person feels that way too, that the more money you got, the less you are going to pay, the more deals that are set up for you to get out of it. It's clear. That's human nature. You get control of things, and then you set it up to help yourself.

Bert's pessimism was extreme:

> How come honesty doesn't mean crap anymore? How come
> sportsmanship is a joke? How come it's okay to be arrested if
> you are a politician, write a book and make a million dollars?
> How come you can be the president of the United States and
> just get pardoned when some guy who's got the wrong skin
> color can do seven, ten years, twenty years in jail for
> nothing? How come? You tell me why. How do you expect
> people to respect the judicial system when the judge is a
> known bigot? He is anti-women?

I cannot overemphasize the depth of corruption these people
saw. The feeling of distrust was absolutely central to all of their
thoughts. It is hard to find a single page in the transcripts of any of
their interviews that does not have some mention of their inability
to trust the government. When I asked Bert what was the most
important problem facing the nation, he said credibility. When I
asked Mark what was the one thing that he would most like to see
changed in the United States, he responded, "To have the people
able to trust the government." When I asked Gail what aspects of
politics interested her, she said, "When sometimes the politicians
say they are going to do something, they get into office and they
don't do it."

Time and again, this corruption was attributed to human nature, to the way things were, to the inevitable power of money.
There was, it seemed, little that could be done. And this, in turn,
led to two distinctive responses. Four of these people – Gus, Howard, Gail, and Dave – responded with almost complete alienation.
None of them voted regularly (though Howard and Dave admitted
to voting occasionally), and none claimed much interest in politics
(Howard and Dave had a limited interest). They talked about corruption with an almost resigned disgust. For example, Howard
discussed his lack of trust in leaders:

> I don't know what the hell we can do. It's been going on for
> years, so what could you do about it? No, I don't trust them.
> They tell you one thing and do the opposite. Like right down
> in Utica, you can see the political leader there has got in

trouble [referring to the local state assemblyperson who had been forced to resign by a sexual abuse scandal]. Right. Of course, we don't hear about the other cities. In every city it's the same.

These four people had very little hope that the problems they saw could be solved. Even when they had a sense that something might be done, they quickly talked themselves out of it. They felt isolated from politics. Gus described what he saw as the problems facing the nation:

It's a tough nut out there in the working world. I wish that our political leaders could turn around and straighten out some of the bullshit that's going on. And that's both within the country and has to do with—I can't say working conditions, but the American manufacturers need a little assistance here and there. But by the same token, they cannot be at the total expense of government, where the leaders of the manufacturing world are making tons and tons of megabucks just because they're supposedly leaders of the industry. Something's got to be revived. Less emphasis on becoming instant millionaires as opposed to turning around and really digging in and just creating something substantial and something that's American-made, American workmanship, American stability. How shall we, say, cut back some of this onslaught of foreign stuff penetrating the market, deteriorating our work force. I don't know. There's things that can be done, but by the same token, there's also too many special interest groups out there that are banging and banging away, can consistently get their handout, even though they're not giving anything for it. You know, like, I'm entitled to it because. And because they sit there on their ass and they make enough noise and they don't go out there and attempt to earn any of it, they're still entitled to it. Something's wrong there. But there's no control.

The other three cynics—Carl, Mark, and Bert—responded not with alienation but with a very conservative political platform. They were skeptical of government activity, they did not believe that social programs would work, and they did not want government interference in their private lives. Mark went so far as to support the Libertarian presidential candidate in the 1976 election. (Interestingly, in 1984 Mark voted for Walter Mondale. When I asked him why, he said there was nothing that he liked about Mondale, but he did not want Reagan to win by too much.) Thus, cynicism seems to lead either to complete alienation or to a desire for very limited government activity. (Some of the alienated cynical individuals do support government activity to solve problems. However, they usually are not optimistic that any of these solutions will work.)

All of the cynics, unlike the skeptics, were distrustful of political activity by citizens. Where the skeptics saw this as a potential way out of the mess the country was in, the cynics, because of their distrust of people in general, did not believe that a more active citizenry would help. Five of them—Bert, Gus, Mark, Gail, and Dave—specifically stated that the vote was meaningless. The other two—Howard and Carl—did not say the vote was meaningless, but they did not have anything positive to say about the ability of citizens to change the way things were. Those in power were bound to abuse that power. There was little that could be done about it. As Mark put it:

> Well, I think you almost got now where you got third- or fourth-generation politicians who just grew up that way, that corruption is part of it. I think basically it's not even considered an honest way of living and working. I think it was back in the 1800s. It's just that corruption, anything, everything gets old, with age, you know. Our Constitution was a great thing, but that was two hundred years ago, and they found a lot of ways around it. It is just human nature. You try to find ways around the rules.

Their distrust also led four of the seven cynics—Bert, Dave, Howard, and Gus—to talk about the importance of keeping "fresh blood" (in Bert's words) in office. As Dave said: "The only way to change [the situation] would be to get other men in there. Once they are in there for ten, twelve years, whatever, it seems like they are so sure of themselves, that they can get away with it, so to speak."

Howard recommended limiting the terms of senators and congressional representatives to eight years because after that, "they get their hands too much in the till down there—they know all the angles." None of the people with other trust orientations made such recommendations.[2]

Five of these people hinted at a conspiracy as an explanation of why things were so bad. Carl, for example, talked about the overwhelming influence of the "Jewish lobby." Mark told me that his mother and he were a little concerned that my interview was a "trap": "That's how they are going to find out how people think so when they come and round you up, they know." (It was only after I convinced him that this was not the case that he agreed to continue the interview.) Bert, when discussing Ronald Reagan as a president, said, "Who knows who is controlling Ronald Reagan? . . . I don't think the president of the United States runs the country or comes close to running it." When I asked him who ran the country, he replied, "Who does run the country? I don't know who runs the country, but I would sure like to know." Dave refused to talk to me about the Kennedy assassination because, "Well, I don't want to stick my head in front of a gun, and that is what it would come down to. They would say, 'There is a guy that is absolutely on the right track,' because my thoughts, I think, are on the right track. So I don't think they would let me live." Gus said: "If we ever get a president in there who's capable of really digging in and cleaning up some of the atrocious messes that are going on, he's not going to survive." Thus, the cynicism of these people led to a conspiratorial explanation for some of what they saw. None of the other people I talked to showed any hint of conspiratorial thinking.

Ironically, the cynics as a group seemed more likely to judge political figures by policy positions than by character, or at least that aspect of character relating to honesty. It was almost as if their distrust of everyone led to them to believe that no one was of superior character or more honest than anyone else. Only Dave and Mark expressed the importance of honesty, as the skeptics did.

Gus, Howard, and Gail mentioned only policies when talking about how they judge a candidate or evaluate political leaders. Gail said the most important factor in deciding who to vote for (on those rare occasions when she did vote) was "what they would do for the American people." She did not mention character or honesty or personality, just helping the public. Howard preferred Reagan to Mondale because Reagan "had a better platform," which Howard said was better in controlling inflation and taxes.

Still, neither Gus nor Gail displayed any strong sense of what policies they preferred. They talked about supporting candidates who would make things better, but they had no sense of what might work. They believed that the answer was not in more honest leaders; hence, that aspect of character was unimportant to them. But, unlike Howard, they did not have a policy orientation toward politics. Rather, their cynicism convinced them that stylistic qualities relating to honesty were irrelevant in making political judgments. To make judgments, they had to look to other qualities or styles.

Carl and Bert used a mixture of policy and character to judge candidates. Carl argued that the two are inseparable:

> It is all tied together, I feel. The policies go along with the man. I mean, as far as the politics, international politics and stuff, how Reagan ran it as opposed to how Carter ran it, it was complete contrast between the two. One of them was the great communicator, and the other guy was nothing. I mean, he was out of touch with the people is how it eventually turned out. And that's why I feel Reagan got the mandate that he got. I mean, I'm not sure, but I think these last two elections with Reagan were the biggest victories in history. I might be wrong as far as U.S. politics is concerned, but he really drubbed him pretty good. But there is the personality of the person, and then there is the policies too.

Both policy and character were important to Bert, but his cynicism ran so deep that he argued that good people would be bad leaders, that we needed people who were dishonest:

> Barry Goldwater said, "Let's go drop a nuclear bomb," and everybody was afraid of him. But they put Richard Nixon in

the White House, who probably was capable of dropping a nuclear bomb, and everybody knew the guy was a son of a bitch. But he was effective, smart. I wouldn't trust him, but he was effective. You know, he was. I think he was effective because the people who knew politics, other politicians who knew politics, feared the man because he was an SOB. He was effective, but I think you got to be in that position.

Thus, the cynics were characterized by an overwhelming distrust of both government and people. They did not believe that political activity would improve the situation, and a number of them did not vote. This distrust often led them to want to limit the time that any leader can spend in office, and it led to more policy-based evaluations of political figures than were found among the skeptics. For the skeptics, honesty in office was crucial. For most of the cynics, honesty was impossible, so the effectiveness of policy became much more important. But effectiveness was highly unlikely. When I asked Mark which of the presidents in his lifetime had been the best, he responded: "I don't think any was that great. Kennedy didn't have much time as president. I don't know. Lyndon Johnson was a crook. And so was Nixon. Nixon was a crook. Ford was just a dummy. Carter was a fish ass. And Reagan puts an act on. So I guess it would have to be Eisenhower because I was too young to dislike him. There's none of them really."

THE SUPPORTERS

Seven people fell into the supporters category: Adam Clay, John Guidry, Nancy Gullet, Tony Hunter, Martha Nettles, Simon Pinella, and Laura Rivers. Their basic orientation was exactly the opposite of the cynics; they trusted both the system and people. They believed that most of our elected officials were honest and tried to do good work, and the system helped keep them that way. It is important within this group to distinguish between those who emphasized the importance of individual trustworthiness (Martha, Nancy, and John) and those who emphasized the role of the system (Simon, Tony, Adam, and Laura).

Martha, Nancy, and John believed that most, if not all, of our political leaders were worthy of our trust. When I asked Nancy who was the best president in her lifetime, she said: "They're all good." Her abiding faith in leadership was reflected in our discussion of Ronald Reagan:

What do you think of Ronald Reagan?

Yes, he is very nice.

Why do you think he's nice?

Well, when he talks on TV, he's a very good man. He wants the best for this country, you see. But some people, they don't pay attention. Some people I hear are not so fine. They don't like him. I say, "Why you don't like him?" I met a woman in the store here in the town, and she says, "Oh, I don't like Reagan." I says, "Why? What's the matter with him? He's nice. He didn't do nothing. He wants what's good for this country."

John said: "[Politicians] are like everyone else. They got the jobs because they enjoy it. They enjoy looking out for the public's interest." And Martha thought we could "trust most of them."

Nancy's trust led to a distancing from politics. Nancy was clearly the most apolitical person I talked to; for her, that was easy, because she believed that things in this country were good. There was little need to take an interest in politics.

Martha, too, was relatively disconnected from politics. She thought that whatever happened in the end was planned: "I think whatever God thinks, whatever God has planned, that's what's going to be." Thus, for her, religious faith led to faith in our leaders. When I asked her what was important in making a voting decision, she said, "Whether or not the president has endorsed them." There is little need to be particularly attentive to politics if our leaders our trustworthy and part of a master plan.

Of the three, John was the most involved in politics, but even his involvement was not particularly high. He paid some attention to what went on, but since most leaders were honest, other factors were crucial in evaluating political figures. The most important factor in making a good leader, to John, was "sternness," their willingness to push hard for what they believed. In evaluating Walter Mondale, John said: "I don't think he was, just in some ways, I just don't think he was powerful enough. I think, more or less, he was a little laid-back, lax." This type of reasoning was reflected in his discussions of a number of other political figures. Those who were not "tough enough," such as Mondale or Jimmy Carter, were not seen favorably. Those that were tough, such as Ronald Reagan or Mario Cuomo, got high marks.

The other four supporters—Simon, Tony, Adam, and Laura—emphasized the positive nature of our political system. Although they basically trusted our leaders, they thought that the system was the key to such trust. Laura, for example, said:

> Well, I think they are trying to do a good job because they were voted in. And I feel that if they weren't voted in, they're going to have to do a good job. Oh, sure, they may be getting something out of it. There's a lot of benefits. But if they were voted in, what else are they going to do.

> *So you think the vote helps keep them honest?*

> I think so. Because they can get out as fast as they got in.

Tony noted that our "government set up rules and regulations . . . for the betterment of the people and is doing a job that you wouldn't say is bad, though it could be better." Simon believed the press was a factor: "The media keeps them honest. If nothing else, the media, though they go too far sometimes, but they keep them honest. We owe that to freedom of the press." Adam, like Laura, argued that "the vote keeps them honest."

These four, then, unlike the three supporters who emphasized the propriety of individuals, thought that political activity by citizens was very important. Keeping the system strong kept our leaders effective. Like the skeptics, these four people believed that citizens should be active in the political arena, (though not all four of them were). As Simon put it:

> [Citizens should be] much more [active] than they are, probably.

Why should they be more active?

Because, I think, by and large, a very small majority of people don't believe their vote counts. They don't believe in becoming involved. And I'm part of it right now, but I'd hate to see the day when nobody's taking any interest in what's happening and then we'll be in trouble. So I think they should play a larger part. And it might call for new commitments by everyone in politics at present and people in general and the media, to get people more involved in local politics, first to see what affects them and then because I think that most people are involved in national politics when they're going for the president. But I'm really not sure how many for congress or senator or state assemblyman or state senator or mayor or councilman or whatever. And I think we were educated about it in middle school in seventh and eighth grade, and by the time you're ready to participate, you forget how the person's elected, or are they voted in or are they appointed or when are they elected, every four, two, six years? So maybe a reeducation to reemphasize the importance of it, something radical to get people more involved in it.

On the whole, however, this group was less active than the skeptics. Perhaps the reason is that their belief in the system was coupled with a basic trust of our political leaders, while the skeptics did not trust those in power. For the skeptics, the pressure to participate in the system was even greater.

These four individuals all found a mix of character and issues to be the most important factor in making evaluations. Tony, for example, said:

I look for a guy that is not too conservative, who is not too liberal. A guy that is not afraid to ask a question. Some guy that does not think he knows it all. Some guy that's not afraid to make a decision. Some guy or some woman, some person, who is willing to give one hundred and ten percent in the position that they're going for, president. Someone that's not there for the prestige about it but is there and wants to do a good job. And then, of course, you have to take in their political views as far as war and foreign aid, foreign policy, domestic policy, and look into their background — what background you can get on them. Are they prejudiced? Financially, are they taking this because they are bored with their life? Are they pompous? Little stuff like that. But you know, I think it all comes down, are they the people that can handle the pressure and make the decisions under the pressure of the job? We're talking a pretty big job. And not only to handle the pressure, but they have to be able to rely somewhat and ask questions of their cabinet, to have a good cabinet and have a good administrative field of advisers so they can get the up-to-date information, the way it's supposed to be done at that time. That can make or break a president, really, if he doesn't have a cabinet that's good.

When describing what she liked about FDR and Harry Truman, Laura mentioned both policy and personal style:

Franklin D. Roosevelt. I just loved that man and what he stood for. His policies, everything he did was right. I mean he had scandals, I think more private than public. That always comes out after a noted person dies, doesn't it? But I think he was my idol. That's when I was first aware of it, back in '36, he ran against Landon. And that's when I started to vote. FDR. Truman wasn't bad. He was kind of in the same mold as FDR, outspoken. But Franklin D. Roosevelt had more finesse. He was more polished.

Adam, too, cited a mix of policy and character traits, noting that the ability to come across to the American people was important. Dynamic speaking ability was one of the traits he looked for in a leader. But he also said it was important that the leader had policies that would benefit the American people. Simon looked for honesty in a president but for the issue positions of congressional candidates. Thus, trust in both the system and most leaders seems to result in an emphasis on character for those who emphasize their trust in people, and in a mixture of policy and character concerns for those whose primary focus is on how the system keeps people honest.

The importance of attitudes toward trust was weaker for this group of individuals than for any of the others. The combination of trust in individuals and trust in the system led to an emphasis on other kinds of factors in the way these people thought about politics. Although most of the other interviews had many unprompted references to issues of trust and honesty, these interviews had very few. Almost all of the comments relating to trust were in direct response to questions about that issue. On reflection, that is not surprising. For all of the other patterns of trust, there is a need to be concerned. Something, either individuals or the system or both, needs watching. Thus, thinking about politics involves thinking about these questions. But for those who fit in the supporters category, trust is taken for granted. Their political thinking, almost by definition, revolves around different things, which leads to a different way of thinking about politics and political issues. These individuals tend either to take their trust to the point that they remove themselves from politics (if they focus on the honesty of individuals) or to support for an active citizenry (if they focus on the effectiveness of the system), though without the fervor and reforming commitment of the skeptics. These supporters tend to look at both the character and the policies of candidates. Most leaders are honest, but the bad apples need to be weeded out or, as in John's case, other personality traits should be examined. The policies that prospective leaders say they are going to follow should be compared because the leaders will, more than likely, attempt to carry out those activities.

At its most extreme, this reservoir of trust can run quite deep. Martha, one of the most supportive of the supporters, shared her thoughts about U.S. policy in Central America:

> Why does the president want to give money to the Contras? Is that right, the Contras? . . . Again, my trust in Reagan. I just feel if he thinks this is the thing to do, then he certainly has all kinds of advisers, and he's intelligent enough himself to know to make a decision. And if this is his decision, boy, I'm with him. Boy, if he thinks we should still be helping this group of people, whichever group of people it is now who are in power or not, I'm for it.

THE "DEMOCRATS"

George Heath, Ralph Randolph, and Ed Stanley fit the final category of trust, what I labeled the democrats. These three men had faith in the system but no faith in politicians.

Their distrust of our leaders ran very deep. When I asked Ralph what he thought was the worst thing about the United States, he answered: "I think it could be some of the politicians." Ed talked about the "dark side of humanity" and the quest for power and money. When I asked George about his interest in politics, he said:

> My interest now in the nationwide scale is, I find it appalling that somehow our congressmen, the page boys. And my first disgust with the national scene — I always felt that once a man became president, no matter if he was Democrat or Republican, he definitely had the thoughts of the people all the time on his side. Now when Agnew pleaded nolo contendere on whatever the charge was, I forget, that disillusioned me. I was real naive, and when they first accused him, I said, "He's right." I kind of liked the guy, and then he pleads that. I said, "Son of a gun." Boy, that smashed me. And then also with the Nixon stuff on the national side. The tapes was all right, the bleep-bleep. I swear a lot. I don't know why I didn't think them people would be *f*-ing this and *f*-ing that. Son of a gun. I always held them in high esteem at that high level. But that's my disillusionment on the national side.

All three of these people expressed a great deal of concern with the honesty of our political leaders, but all of them also expressed faith in the system. In George's words: "It seems to me like, if it does get corrupt, it gets corrupt so much that finally people who are apathetic most of the time finally get together and throw the guy out or whatever, throw the party out." Ed put it this way: "The system is good with people voting. And that's your voice, because it is majority rule. It may be only one vote, but one day your local trustee or congressman or senator will do the wrong thing. Fifty-one percent of the people won't like him for it, and they will vote against him. He'll only get forty-nine percent of the vote, and he will lose."

Ralph argued that elections influenced the behavior of political leaders: "[Politicians] will go ahead and stick their foot out a little farther and say, 'Well, we can do this. We can do that.' Hopefully, they will try to do it."

All of these people believed that political activity was crucial. The system needed to function to prevent crooked politicians from hurting the nation. Ed and George had been active in politics, working for candidates. Ed noted: "I think it is the doubt every two years or four years that keeps politicians more honest than they are, if they are honest. It keeps them a little honest." Thus, he argued, people should be active and vote. When he worked in campaigns, he would tell people, "Go in the booth. At least go vote. Go in and vote. Vote against me. But go."

Ralph, however, had not been active. He explained this seeming contradiction in this way:

Do you think it would make a difference if more people voted?

I don't know if it would change the way [leaders] acted. It might change their views, maybe. Like I say I haven't voted, but I think myself that everybody should vote. . . . I think the people are the ones that speak for our country, America. If everybody went out and voted, there would be a better chance of more people getting what they like or what they thought they liked.

So you think it does make a difference?

I would say so. Definitely I would say so. If people got out and voted, it would.

And why do you think a lot of people don't vote?

Because they say, "Why should I vote? Ain't nothing in it for me." It's, I think, the wrong attitude. You get together and want something, you're going to get it, or you are going to have a chance at it anyway. Why give the other guy the power at the ballot anyway? Let them win? You don't care. You don't like it anyways, but you are letting them win, so I think if more people got together, and everybody was to vote, and then this world would be a little better anyways. I think more people, when they probably want it, and even if they lost, they still would be able to try. Yeah, I think so. There's a lot of people that don't though. I think it's the majority, this attitude that people carry with them: "Well, there is not enough information, so I'm not going to vote." Well, like this attitude I had when Reagan was running against Mondale, right? So I don't know much about either one. I don't really care all that much for Reagan. But I'm not going to vote for either one. So there you go. As I said, I don't care for Reagan, but I didn't know much about Mondale.

The democrats, then, believed in democracy. Unlike the skeptics, they did not emphasize reforming the system to make it better. Rather, they simply thought people needed to use the system more. Still, their fear of political leaders led to some desire for change. Ed, for example, thought that laws should be written very precisely, to prevent politicians from interpreting them in ways that only serve their own interests. George and Ed decried the influence of lobbyists, though neither recommended campaign finance reform as a solution. Ed said: "The system will work. It can work. It does work really. I feel special interest groups are a problem." George noted that "these special interest groups are having a lot of effect." But the "democrats" believed that these problems could be overcome if people got involved.

This pattern of beliefs leads to an emphasis on character in evaluating political figures, though these evaluations seem to be more policy-oriented than those of the skeptics. Ralph, for example, thought Jimmy Carter was a better president than Ronald Reagan : "He listened a little better, and he had a better ear listening to problems. And I think unemployment wasn't as bad then as it is now." George explained what traits he looked for:

I think past performance is one. Whatever publicity they give to new contenders, hopefully you can grab something out of it — what they will do, good or bad, good or whatever. I have no faith in platforms, whatever they put down. And then how they come over on TV. I think that damn charisma probably affects me subconsciously. I think I go past performance, and the new candidates, whatever they say about them.

Why don't you think you can go by the platform?

I don't think they, not that I can remember distinctly every platform, but I don't think they—I recollect I read this a couple of years ago—they never adhere to them, the platforms. They have them, but that's it. They certainly don't put the weight on them like they do when they are trying to sell them when they are beginning to run. Platforms, I also believe, are just to get the most people, representative types of people. You know, union types, give you something about unions.

Ed noted: "Jimmy Carter was not a leader . . . a person who believes in what he believes in and will do it." But he also stated that when choosing between Carter and Reagan, more than the ability to lead came into play: "I listened to Ronald Reagan when he was running for office against Jimmy Carter. I listened to Jimmy Carter when he was running for office. I heard both of their speeches. I just heard intelligence that I had learned in college in my economics courses and my business courses coming out of Ronald Reagan's mouth."

Thus, character was important to the democrats. What kind of a person was in office mattered, but because most leaders were not honest, policy and performance also mattered. Still, the most striking feature of this group was the centrality of their disillusionment with our leaders. Despite a belief in the system and its ability to make things work, this group profoundly distrusted people in power, and that distrust was central to how they thought about politics. Like the involved cynics, attitudes toward trust were present in almost every answer that these people gave. They trusted the system but not our leaders. It was not that good people did not exist; if that were the case, they would not have had their faith in the vote. But good people did not usually get involved in politics. In fact, they should not. As George said, "Incidentally, I wouldn't let my sons work for the government. I wouldn't let Bob, my

Roger[3]. Oh, God. Oh, no. I don't believe it. And there is a lot of good people, but it is not for real good people. They should not go there."

The role of trust

The relationship of these attitudes to various demographic and basic political factors is not particularly revealing, but a few patterns are worth noting. First, the cynics tended to be less educated than the other groups. Four of the six individuals in the study who did not have a high school degree fell into this category. Education did not preclude cynicism (one of the cynics, Bert, had an advanced degree), but it did seem to have some effect.

Second, in terms of partisanship, five of the seven cynics were independents. This was not surprising, because we would expect a general cynicism to be coupled with cynicism about the parties. The other group with a large number of independents was the three supporters. Four of the seven individuals in this category had no party identification. Interestingly, these four included three supporters who focused on their trust of all individuals (as opposed to focusing on their trust of the system). Again, those who emphasized the uniformity of individuals, who thought of people as all good or all bad, seemed to see little difference between the parties.

Perhaps the most interesting relationship was that between the liberal-conservative orientation and trust orientation.[4] For the most part, those who trusted the system (the democrats and the supporters) had stylistic orientations toward liberals and conservatives, while those who did not trust the system (the cynics and the skeptics) had policy orientations or, in the case of the cynics, no orientation at all (see table 3.2).

Of the seven supporters, five had stylistic orientations, one had no orientation, and only one had a policy orientation. Of the three democrats, two had stylistic orientations, and the other had a combined stylistic and policy orientation. On the other hand, of the seven cynics, three had no ideological orientation at all, two had policy orientations, and two had combined policy and stylistic orientations. Of the nine skeptics, five had policy orientations, one had no orientation, and three had stylistic orientations. Clearly the

Table 3.2. Relationship between interviewees' trust orientation and ideological orientation

Ideological orientation	Trust orientation				Total
	Cynic	Skeptic	"democrat"	Supporter	
None	3	1	0	1	5
Style	0	3	2	5	10
Style and policy	2	0	1	0	3
Policy	2	5	0	1	8
Total	7	9	3	7	26

Note: Figures are the numbers of interviewees fitting each category.

relationship is not perfect, but it does seem to be present. Those who trusted the system seemed to define the ideology of people by their style, while those who did not trust the system relied on a policy analysis to categorize people as liberals or conservatives.

In part, this fits what we have seen in terms of how trust orientation relates to the broader types of evaluations people make. Supporters and democrats relied on character evaluations, and cynics relied on issue evaluations, which matches their liberal-conservative orientation. However, the skeptics do not fit. Skeptics seemed to rely on character evaluations to judge candidates, but they also tended to have policy orientations when it came to their liberal-conservative orientation. Perhaps this is explained by the relatively high education of the skeptics (seven of the nine had at least some college, and five were college graduates, some with advanced degrees). Education might allow them to distinguish the policy basis of liberal-conservative distinctions, but their skepticism led them to rely on character judgments when evaluating individual leaders. It is difficult with only twenty-six people to sort out the relationships present, but for now we need to note the relationship between trust orientation and liberal-conservative orientation. We will return to these issues in the final chapter when we take a closer, more general look at stylistic and policy orientations toward politics.

These attitudes toward trust, then, underlie many of the other attitudes that people have. For example, one of the questions I asked people had to do with the tax reform legislation that was then being discussed.[5] Because this bill was not yet in its final form when we discussed it, the basic orientation that people had toward politics played a major role in shaping their impressions. Clearly, other factors shaped support or opposition to tax reform, but it is also clear that the underlying attitude of trust shaped the way these people thought about the proposed changes.

The cynics, by and large, were cynical about the bill. Four of the seven said they were opposed to it because it would make things worse. The others said they did not know anything about the proposal. (One of these three, Mark, was opposed to any income tax at all.) They did not believe any reform would really help.

The skeptics, on the other hand, were split. Two of the nine did not know anything about the proposal, two were supportive of the bill, and one was opposed to it. The other four were skeptical. They knew of the bill but were not sure what effect it would have. As Walter said, "I think it will probably be about the same. We will all be in the same boat."

The supporters were supportive of tax reform in general. This group was the least informed about the proposal, with five of the seven saying they did not know anything about the bill. That fit with the relatively trusting and removed attitudes that characterize this group. The two who did know about it supported it. Interestingly, of the five who did not know about it, Laura thought that "they were probably trying to help," and Martha, Adam, and Nancy expressed the view that the current tax system was relatively fair anyway (they were the only people in the entire sample to express such a view). Only one, John, registered dissatisfaction with the tax system in general.

All three of the democrats were split on the bill. They thought it was a good idea but worried about whether special interests could be kept out of the battle. As Ed put it: "One of the things I like about the new tax laws is that they are happening without special interests getting involved, although I can see a lot of it happening that they are." From this perspective, if the system could be kept free of corrupting influences, it could do some good, but a danger that the bill could turn out badly was clearly present.

Thus, orientation toward trust helped shape the way that these people thought about political issues. I am not arguing that we can explain attitudes on tax reform by trust orientation. The relationship is clearly not so simple or direct. Other influences also play an important role. But trust orientation does affect the way that people think about the issue, and in that sense it is central to the way people think about politics.

Conclusions

These different patterns of trust, then, lead to different ways of thinking about politics. For example, the factors people rely on to make political evaluations are partially a function of their trust orientation. Skeptics rely primarily on character judgments (or at least, when making character judgments, they emphasize honesty), cynics rely more on policy orientations, and supporters and democrats rely on a combination of character judgments and policy orientations, though both groups tend to rely more on character.

Skeptics and democrats are also strong believers in the need for political activity, though their orientation toward the system leads skeptics to desire activity that will change the system, while democrats simply want to use the system as it is. Supporters also support political activity, but their level of trust makes it less central to their view of how the system can be made effective, and in some cases it even allows them to withdraw from the system completely. Cynics, on the other hand, are skeptical of the ability of political activity to have any influence at all, and this in turn leads them to withdraw from the system too (though in a much more alienated fashion than the withdrawn supporters, the most cynical skeptics lapsing into a conspiratorial explanation of politics that precludes any individual from exercising influence) or to support a political agenda of very limited government activity.

It is interesting to note how trust orientations that are opposite can have similar behavioral consequences or lead to similar attitudes on other topics. Both supporters and cynics can end up withdrawing from the system, though for very different reasons. Similarly, both democrats (who trust the system) and skeptics (who do not) support an active citizenry. If we simply ask people whether they think the vote is important, we miss these very different roots. The differences in trust orientation have enormous implications for the meaning of people's belief in political activity. The distinction between trust in the system and trust in our leaders is an important one. We need to be clear about which type of trust is motivating people toward political activity. Cynics' disgust leads them not to vote; supporters do not vote because they think things will turn out okay in the end anyway. Skeptics vote because they want to elect people to change the system; democrats vote because they like the system as it is and think we need to use it to protect ourselves from corrupt leaders. If we want to analyze a decline or rise in participation or activity or trust, we need to be careful to distinguish these different patterns. It is not enough to say there has been a decline in trust in the system or a decline in trust in our leaders. Rather, we need to explore the interaction of these two types of trust.[6]

Trust orientation is an important factor in shaping how people approach politics. It helps them make sense of the political world by giving them cues about how much faith to put into political leaders or proposed solutions. Cynics, for example, when they are politically involved, are likely to support very limited government. Since they trust neither the system nor our leaders, nothing else makes much sense. Similarly, skeptics worry that the system will corrupt the ability of people to solve problems and therefore are likely to support activities designed to reform the system. If they find a leader they trust, they are likely to support any changes, no matter how large, that leader proposes. The problem they see is not leadership—we have good leaders—but those leaders are often dragged down by the corrupt system. Thus, when someone "good" calls for a new policy, the skeptics will, at least initially, be supportive.

In contrast, democrats are skeptical of leaders. Thus, they are likely to support strict rules and regulations that tie the hands of leaders. They believe that keeping a tight reign on people is the only way to keep the system working fairly.

For supporters, trust orientation is relatively unimportant. Although each of the other three groups takes their attitude toward either the system or our leaders (or both) into account when making sense of politics, supporters, because of their complete trust, are freed from such considerations. I found cynics, democrats, and skeptics raising issues of trust in one form or another regularly during the course of our discussions, but supporters rarely raised these issues except upon direct questioning. In making sense of politics, trust was something they simply took for granted.

However, trust orientation is not sufficient to allow people to make sense of the political world. This is clearly the case with supporters, but it is also true of skeptics, democrats, and most cynics. (For the most cynical of the cynics, cynicism may explain just about all of their attitudes. They trust no one, and nothing is likely to make things better. But such complete alienation and cynicism is likely to be rare.) Trust orientation does shape the kinds of things people take into account when they look at the system, our leaders, or policy proposals. It does help people make sense of politics. If people have faith in the system, they react differently to politics than people who do not. If they have faith in leaders, they respond differently to them and their suggestions than people who do not. But other orientations underlying political views also help people make sense of politics. We will examine these other orientations in the next two chapters.

The scope of politics

Now Main Street's whitewashed window and vacant stores
seems like there ain't nobody wants to come down
here no more
They're closing down the textile mill across
the railroad tracks
Foreman says these jobs are going boys and they ain't
coming back to your hometown
Your hometown

—BRUCE SPRINGSTEEN

"Kathy," I said,
As we boarded a Greyhound in Pittsburgh,
"Michigan seems like a dream to me now.
It took me four days
To hitchhike from Saginaw.
I've come to look for America."

—PAUL SIMON

We are the world.

—MICHAEL JACKSON and LIONEL RICHIE

A second factor that underlies the way people try
to make sense of politics is how broadly or narrowly they tend to
view the political world. That is, for some people politics is largely
a matter of local concerns, while for others it is a national affair.
And for some it is a matter of America's place in the world; politics
takes on an international flavor.

As with an individual's trust orientation, the scope that people
define for their political world underlies the way they make sense

of political events. There are a few people for whom this factor seems to make little difference; they recognize and deal with politics on all of these levels, and they do not seem to give higher priority to any one of the levels. But for most, their vision of the scope of politics is an important factor in shaping how they make sense of politics.

Local visions of politics

For eight of the people I spoke with, politics primarily revolved around local concerns: Gail Blair, Al Chambliss, Sue Doyle, Howard Gossage, Ted Munson, Ed Stanley, Gus White, and Carla Zeber. For four of them—Ed, Al, Gus, and Ted—this vision came from a commitment to the idea that they could have more influence on the local level. For example, when I asked Ted about his interest in politics, he said:

> I am sort of interested in politics at two levels. I'm interested in local politics at a far different level than national politics. I don't have much of a belief that what happens nationally politically is going to make that much difference to what happens to me as a citizen of Utica, New York. So I vote, I pay attention to what's going on, and I write nasty letters to my congressman and my senators and to Mr. Reagan, but I see that differently than I see people like the mayor of Utica and the local legislature and people like that. . . . I think it also has something to do with the fact that Utica politics, itself, are so colorful. That makes it more interesting. It doesn't seem that a day goes by when something crazy doesn't happen with the local politicians. Whether it be our fearless leaders on the water board who are getting ready to have a fight at the water board meeting, or whether it's the fact that the snow hasn't been plowed and things like that. I think it's closer to home. And it's something that I think maybe I can have something to say about.

Al noted that he was more interested in local politics because "that's where I have the greatest influence," and Ed, in discussing areas where government spending could be cut, noted: "I am not condemning liberal social programs or food for Africa, but I guess what I see as the threat is C Street in Utica."[1] Gus said: "When we turn around and start considering national politics, which is down in Washington, D.C., we're so far away from that. You know that we have a spokesman and a representative and so on and so forth, but I don't think there is that close a pipeline to a federal level. No way in hell."

Three of these four men talked about their ability to influence local politics in a way they could not influence national level politics. All three were conversant with national political issues, but such issues were not a focus of their political world. Gus was the one exception. He did not feel particularly capable of influencing politics at any level, though he clearly paid much closer attention to what happened locally. More important, the beliefs of these four people reflected this feeling of the primacy of local interests. Ted, a liberal Democrat with generally liberal political views, said he supported Alphonse D'Amato because of D'Amato's ability to get things done for New York State, and he also noted that the most important job of members of Congress is to help their local constituencies. All four men expressed a commitment to returning more control to state and local government. For example, after expressing support for local control over welfare policies and speed limits, Ed said: "Is the federal government so right and the state government so wrong that the state is going to do something crazy? I mean, I just don't know why the federal government needs such tremendous control over the states. The federal government doesn't know either."

These four, then, have a commitment to local politics that arises from a view of where they can be most influential. The other four individuals with a local orientation have less conscious reasons for it. But it is clear from talking with them that politics is primarily a local phenomenon. For example, when I asked Howard what kinds of things he found most interesting about politics, he said: "I want to see where all of our money is going to New York City instead of upstate New York where it's supposed to belong." When I asked him what we could do about that he told me they should "make New York City a state of its own, put a fence right there." In Howard's view, local problems were the ones that needed to be solved. What was happening elsewhere in the country or even the state didn't matter much. That was their problem. He even suggested sending people on welfare in New York State back to the state of their birth ("Why should they come up and live off us?").

Similarly, Carla and Gail have an interest only in local issues. Carla discussed the sewer tax, local education, and the need to keep industries in the area, but she had no real sense of, or opinions on, national political issues. Gail talked at length about city codes, cleaning up the streets of Utica, and the local police and fire departments and was familiar with all of her city and state representatives and what they had or had not done for the area. On the other hand, she claimed ignorance about the job that New York's U.S. senators and her local member of Congress had done, noting, "I never pay no attention."

Sue's interest was even more limited than what happened locally. For Sue, what was important was family. She was concerned with her role as a mother. As was noted in the last chapter, Sue had no trust in government to do anything anyway, and she therefore opposed most government programs. However, she found a few family-related things useful:

> The library. There are government-funded programs, I can tell, that give money to the library and are now putting on for the children in the summertime. Yeah, that's where I see tax dollars. I don't need it with my daughter. I've always brought her to the library. Books are a wonderful thing and whatever. But I am sure that there are a lot of families that don't do what we do. And it encourages kids, and that's good. We go to the library, and I take her to the programs. And in school they had — I think it was state-funded — some contest where you read so many books with your parent, with a partner for reading. And you didn't have to do it, but if you did, you got some kind of prize or gift or whatever. That's good. Those kind of things. We don't need them, but I guess other people do, and if it's going to benefit, I guess that's good.

Sue talked at length about education, the library, the local environment (in particular, water quality and garbage disposal), but she did not have much at all to say about most national political issues (except to oppose government spending) and no opinion on most international issues. She stated that what was important to her was not politics: "[Politics] is just not my thing. There are other things that are much more important to me right now. I'm a mother, developing our child." But that perspective led her to focus on a few local political issues that she did not even see as politics. In her mind, those issues were family-related.

For these eight individuals, then, the focus of politics was local. In some cases that focus was a result of a conscious decision that arose from a belief in where the individual was likely to have an impact, and in other cases it arose from a more unconscious development of local priorities. But in all cases this orientation affected the way these people made sense of the political world. What happened at the local level was their primary focus. They judged political outcomes, events, and figures by their effect on the local community. Three of these people—Al, Ed, and Ted—were quite conversant with national and, to a lesser extent, international political issues. The other five had little sense of such events and issues. For all eight the local impact was the primary focus. That was not the case for those with a national political orientation.

National visions of politics

Eight people had national visions of politics: Walter Beattie, Mark Dent, Nancy Gullet, Tony Hunter, Mort Johnson, Clyde Lyle, Ralph Randolph, and Carol Torrez. For them, politics was largely a function of what went on at the national level. For example, Nancy talked about problems with the local economy, noting that her grandson was having a hard time finding a job. But at the same time, she thought that Ronald Reagan was a good president because things in the country were going well and because the president "wants what's good for the country."

The problems that these people tended to focus on were much broader than those mentioned by people with local orientations. In discussing economic problems, Carol said: "I don't think today, in all honesty, I can say the government is paying that much attention, when I think of the unemployed steel workers in Pennsylvania, for example, which you've also got in Ohio and other Midwest states. When I think of the farmers' plight in the Midwest, to say nothing of the farmers in the Southeast right now."

The focus was on national, not local, issues and problems. Two of these people, Ralph and Nancy, had little knowledge of political issues at any level, in Ralph's case because of an alienation from politics and in Nancy's case because of a basic trust in our leaders to do what is right. But both clearly focused on national standards and issues. To the extent that they did talk about politics, it was national politics that they had opinions about.

This tendency was even clearer for the other six individuals in this category. All of them were relatively conversant with some national political issues, offering opinions and ideas about those issues but expressing little or no interest in local issues. Tony, in fact, noted that he didn't follow city politics as much as national politics.

People with a local orientation often noted what their local representatives had done for the district. For those with a national orientation, however, the focus was on where the representative stands on national issues. Clyde, for example, judged all political figures by where they stood on social issues such as abortion and crime. And Walter, in discussing the role of a member of Congress, said: "I think if you solve national problems, you also solve the problems of your constituency. So I think you can't just be concerned with your constituency. . . . It's too narrow to just think of your own small area as opposed to the nation."

Mort also complained that some representatives "are interested in the home territory to the expense of the global, national picture." Carol, while discussing her state senator and his apparent popularity, complained:

> [The people] know that Senator [James] Donovan is a nice guy. We meet him and are pleased, and he has done a lot for around here and roads and things. [The state legislators] are all doing a lot for their people, so nobody wants to open up on the guy. He's a neighbor. I guess that's the big thing. But they are taking people, the State of New York, for a ride.

Doing well locally was not enough for people in this group. Judgments were made on broader grounds. Most of these people also discussed international affairs, especially Mark, Tony, Ralph, and Clyde, but again that was not their focus. Ralph, in fact, made the comparison explicitly. He said he thought Ronald Reagan conducted foreign policy far more effectively than Jimmy Carter had, but he preferred Carter as president because Carter "was a little better with this country."

Thus, for these eight people, the focus of politics was national. They were most conversant with national political issues, and they tended to judge political figures by their opinions on, or performance with regard to, national issues, not local (or global) concerns. This attitude affected the way they made sense of politics. Probably the best example of this was Clyde, an individual who, as we have seen, was very conservative in most of his political positions. On the other hand, his national focus left him in the nonconservative habit of believing that problems should be dealt with at the national, not the local, level. He supported the idea of national regulation of business for environmental and health reasons (though he thought they currently overregulate), and he told me he could not think of any policy areas in which the national government was involved but should not be. He clearly supported the conservative view that there should be less government, but this view was mixed with a national focus that caused him to think that if government was to be involved, it was probably better to have national, rather than state or local, regulations.

A national focus is aided by the use of information sources other than the local papers and the local news. All of these people, except Mark, specifically mentioned the network newscasts, national news magazines, or the *New York Times* as their major source of information about politics. In contrast, only one of the people with local orientations (Ted) cited such a source. The local-orientation group most often mentioned local papers or local newscasts as their major information source.[2]

Thus, for this group of eight people, making sense of politics involved sorting out national issues and how the nation as a whole was doing. This is not to say that they did not have any interest in local or international events. They did. But when they thought about political problems and issues, and whether they support or oppose political figures, the context of their thoughts was a national one. For them, politics was about what was happening in the United States.

International visions of politics

I was somewhat surprised to find that five of the people I talked with seemed to have an international view of politics. Given the low level of information that many Americans have about international affairs, I would not have expected that almost one-fifth of the people I talked to would have such a view.[3] For Carl Figueroa, John Guidry, Martha Nettles, Simon Pinella, and Dave Thomasson, politics was played out in the world arena, and these five people exhibited two distinct outlooks.

Simon, Martha, and Dave displayed a view of the world as one large family. Simon, for example, said: "It's divisions among people and boundaries that cause war. Where if you're all helping each other, I sometimes think if we ever had a threat from another planet, we wouldn't think of ourselves as Americans. We'd think of earthlings or whatever. So maybe if we can get more of an earthling mentality and promote it, it'd be significant."

Martha and Dave also discussed the need for all the nations of the world to get along in peace. For both of them, this focus sprang from their religious faith. They talked about the whole planet's being part of God's plan and about our need to think of all of the world as belonging to God.

Neither Martha nor Dave had much knowledge of specific foreign-policy issues, but they both focused on international events in discussing politics. Martha, for example, expressed bewilderment at how people from other nations could think badly of the United States: "How can these countries' heads of states possibly say that Eisenhower and Kennedy and Johnson and Carter and Reagan were warmongers? I just don't possibly understand how they could say that." She clearly judged political events by how they affected world peace. Watergate, for example, was a tragedy because of how it made us look in the eyes of the rest of the world and how that made peace more difficult. Similarly, she judged presidents by her view of their efforts for achieving peace: "I certainly think the president should be mostly concerned with keeping peace with the other countries. I realize that keeping the economy right here at home so that everyone has a job, I realize how important that is. That to me is not quite as important as the United States, being respected throughout the world."

For Martha, achieving world peace was the focus of politics. She supported anything or anyone who she thought would help that cause. The same was true of Dave. The one issue that aroused his ire was putting weapons in space. He mentioned a number of times that God wanted us to deal with our problems on earth, and we should not contaminate space in any way. The way to achieve peace and understanding on earth was not through putting weapons, or anything else, in space.

Simon, on the other hand, was much more clearly informed about a broad range of foreign-policy issues. He followed international affairs closely and was noticeably excited to talk about such topics as South Africa, Central America, and U.S.-Soviet relations. He was concerned that "we do a bad job, in particular, by not emphasizing the rest of the world more to Americans" and that our politicans "don't pay enough attention to the rest of the world either."

In contrast to these three, Carl and John did not view the world as potentially one big family. Rather, they saw the world as a hostile place where America was largely surrounded by enemies. For them, the focus of politics was also international affairs, but what was most important was maintaining the strength and prestige of the United States so that we could prosper and defeat our enemies.

Carl had more interest in and knowledge of foreign affairs than anyone else I talked with:

> [I like] to know where America stands as far as which countries fall, who's got this, who's got that. The fighting, like in South Yemen — I'm keeping track of that. The different governments that Afghanistan had. Yeah, I like to know what's going on. I like to know how much closer they are. I'm not superparanoid, don't get me wrong, as far as them closing right up on our borders and this kind of thing. But I like to know more or less what's ours and what's theirs.

Needless to say, he was the only one I talked to who mentioned South Yemen! For Carl, keeping America strong was the key: "If you let yourself fall, eventually your enemies are going to take advantage of it. And then these freedoms that we have, you're going to lose them." Consequently, he judged politics in terms of how policies and actions would affect America's place in the world. Leaders needed to make America a strong nation. If they failed at that, they were inviting disaster.

John had a similar perspective, but without Carl's detailed knowledge of, or intense interest in, international affairs. John liked living in "the strongest country around." He too judged our leaders by whether they were able to maintain or increase the country's strength. He liked Richard Nixon, in spite of Watergate, because of his foreign policy, and Ronald Reagan was a good leader because he protected the United States from foreign threats.

John even tended to see domestic economic issues in a foreign context. Two of the major problems he saw with the economy were unfair foreign competition and the large number of immigrants dragging down wages. John thought we needed to close our borders both to immigrants and to imports. The world was a hostile place, and we needed to fight to maintain our place in it.

For these five people, politics was international. They judged political events and figures by their impact on America's place in the world, either in terms of how we could achieve peace or how we could maintain our strength. But despite their international focus, only one of these people, Carl, displayed a great deal of knowledge of the details of foreign affairs, and only two others, Simon and John, were somewhat conversant with foreign policy. Dave and Martha were largely unaware of the details of international events, but international events were important to their worldview. All of these people tended to make sense of politics through a vision of how the world should look. They were less concerned with their local area or state or nation than with the entire world. Thus, the conduct of international affairs was their prime concern. They tended to make sense of politics through a very broad lens.

Mixed visions of politics

Five people could not be classified as fitting into any one of these categories. Three of them—Adam Clay, George Heath, and Laura Rivers—had a mixture of national and local orientations.

Adam tended toward a national perspective. He was concerned with national issues and had no real interest in local politics. On the other hand, he supported giving more power to the states and he thought the job of members of Congress was to "try and appropriate funds to get projects done in their area . . . try and bring money into his area." Because Adam was attending college away from home, it may be that his interest in local politics was undeveloped because of a lack of a strong tie to a single community. But in any case, he seemed to display elements of both national and local orientations.

Laura also offered a mix of these orientations. She did not display much knowledge of either national or local issues, and she seemed to judge political leaders by their effects on both the nation and the local community. She maintained that it was important for representatives to do good things for their district, and she expressed concern that the country had gotten too big: "It's just too large. Of course, our country has gotten so big, from the thirteen colonies right up to Alaska and Hawaii now. How much further can we go? And we're just a little cog in the wheel, I think now. I say, as long as I have a warm bed, a roof over my head, and food in my refrigerator, I'm happy. But that's not speaking for all the other millions. I think small, I guess. I'm not looking for anything."

On the other hand, in judging politics she often expressed concern for "the other millions," making it impossible to call her orientation entirely local. She also tended to look at economic issues from a national rather than local perspective. Laura came close to having a local orientation, but there was too much of a national focus in her views to put her in that category.

The same was true for George. In many ways George had an extremely local orientation. He was fascinated by local politics. He paid a great deal of attention to what went on at the local level, following local events and figures. And he said: "I would vote for almost any presidential candidate that came from New York State. I would feel that they would think of us more."

On the other hand, George also displayed a national perspective. He said members of the House of Representatives should look to see if a policy is "good for the country," not just their district, but he also believed that on issues other than defense and the economy, they should fight for their constituencies. His evaluation of political figures was based on national as well as local benchmarks.

The fourth individual with a mixed perspective was Amy Tidrow. Her mixture was of national and international perspectives. She was concerned with "our relations with other countries" and said: "I am more interested in that stuff than a lot of current events." She clearly looked to see how various activities affected our standing in the world. On the other hand, she did not display the same kind of focus that those with a purer international perspective exhibited. Her evaluations of political figures, for example, were more tied in with national events and issues, such as the economy. She said a member of Congress should look out for the welfare of the whole nation, an attitude that was prevalent among those with a national perspective. In addition, she expressed ignorance about the actual conduct of the United States on most foreign-policy issues. She said she had "heard a few things" about South Africa but really did not have any opinion, and that she knew "more about South Africa than I do about Nicaragua." In sum, she displayed a largely national perspective but had a stronger sense of the importance (though not the details) of foreign policy than those with a clearer national focus.

Finally, there was Bert Jackson. His focus could best be described as cynical at all levels. He did not like or trust local politicians or national figures. He was alienated from what our leaders did locally, nationally, and internationally. He believed that the federal government should give some power back to the states, but he didn't trust the state government either. A number of times he expressed the view that "the worst thing about politics is the fact that no one knows anything about politics to give you an accurate description of what's wrong with the system." His complete cynicism about politics at all levels made it impossible to determine whether his primary orientation was local, national, or international.

Causes and consequences
of the broadness of scope

The roots of these orientations are not very clear. The only demographic factor that seems to play any role at all is education, and that role is limited. Four of the six people without a high school degree had a local orientation (see table 4.1). Thus, it seemed that those with limited education were more likely to focus on local politics. On the other hand, greater education did not seem to lead to a broader scope. College graduates were split equally among local, national, and international perspectives, and the three people who had advanced degrees were divided, with one having a national perspective (Mort), one having a local perspective (Ted), and one who did not adopt any particular orientation (Bert).

Table 4.1. Relationship between interviewees' scope orientation and education

| Education | Scope orientation | | | | |
	Local	National	International	Mixed	Total
Grade school	1	1	1	0	3
Some high school	3	0	0	0	3
High school	1	1	2	1	5
Some college	0	3	0	3	6
College	2	2	2	0	6
Advanced degree	1	1	0	1	3
Total	8	8	5	5	26

Note: Figures are the numbers of interviewees fitting each category.

Interest in politics, partisanship, and ideology all seem to be unrelated to the broadness of ones scope of politics, at least as far as we can tell from a group of twenty-six people. Thus, scope orientation does not seem to be related to any systematic demographic differences, with the possible exception of education. The reasons for the development of such orientations seem to be more closely related to the individual life experiences that people have. The clearest examples of this were the three people (Ted, Ed, and Al) who consciously focused on local politics because of their feeling that they could have more influence at that level. Similarly, the local vision of less-educated citizens may reflect the more limited worlds that they tend to live in. Education tends to broaden one's experiences but does not always lead to a broader vision of politics. Without higher education, however, it does seem more difficult to develop a national or international perspective on politics.

In other cases, the impact of life experiences was more indirect. The two college students, for example, did not show much of a local orientation. Adam had some elements of localism in his views, but no real locality to which he could relate, and Amy mixed national and international perspectives. Clyde, who had just graduated from college, had a national orientation. It is difficult while in college to develop any strong attachment to the hometown or the school community. This might be less difficult if those two communities were the same, but in these three cases, home and school were in different places.

Thus, many of those with a national orientation, found little of relevance in local politics. They did not pay much attention to local newscasts or papers, preferring the network news and/or national news magazines. For those with a local orientation, on the other hand, national politics seemed remote. (Sue's commitment to family was a further example of this.)

For those with an international perspective, life experiences also seemed to play a role. Carl, the most interested in foreign affairs, had developed that interest during the Vietnam War. According to him, he almost signed up to go and fight when he realized that the United States was not fighting the war "properly." If we were going to fight, we should have fought to win, something he still believed we "could have done." (On the other hand, the two Vietnam veterans I talked with, Tony and Mark, had national, not international, perspectives, although the war greatly influenced the way they sorted through politics.)

The worldview of Martha and Dave sprang from their religious beliefs. Although Simon did not directly relate his views on the need for world peace to religious convictions, he did tell me that religion was important to him and that he attended church every week.

There is much more to say about how the life experiences that people have affect their political perspectives and the way they make sense of politics, and we will return to these issues in Chapter 6. The point I want to make here is that life experiences seem to shape how broadly people visualize politics — whether they see politics as primarily a local, national, or international phenomenon.

The consequences of different perspectives on the scope of politics were clearer. For one thing, these perspectives led to different types of judgments about political figures and events. Those with a local perspective were more likely to judge political events and figures by their impact on the local community, so conservative localists might support a liberal member of the House in their district if that member took care of the district, or vice versa.

People with a national or international perspective, on the other hand, were much less likely to make such judgments. They were more concerned with national or international trends and events. Those with a national perspective were concerned with how the nation was doing, while those with an international perspective focused on how the nation fit into the world.

Additionally, the focus that people had affected the types of issues they saw as important. Those with a national perspective, for example, were more likely to look at the national economy when evaluating an incumbent president. Those with a local perspective were most likely to be concerned with how things in their community were going; the local community was much more likely to be seen as a test of national success or failure. Those with an international perspective focused on the country's standing in the world. For them, even national issues were important because they affected our international standing. A scandal in an administration, for example, would be important because of how it would make us look in the eyes of the world.

I do not want to give the impression that these perspectives mean that citizens judge political leaders by their positions on issues at the appropriate level. As we have seen, some citizens do not think much about issues at all. Rather, their concerns are with styles of politics. Thus, someone with a stylistic sense of politics and a local orientation toward it will want leaders who have the right kind of style to solve problems at the local level (whatever that style may be). Similarly, those with an international perspective may find a particular style of foreign policy to be effective. Those worried about America's place in a hostile world and those who stress our need to live together will want different styles of leadership.

On the other hand, because citizens tend to pay attention to particular levels of politics, their information levels often vary depending upon their interest in the level under consideration. Those with a local perspective tend to know more about local political issues and leaders, those with a national perspective tend to know more about national figures, and those with an international perspective tend to know more about foreign-policy issues. This means that some citizens will be more ignorant about politics at levels other than the one to which they are oriented. Because the other levels are usually not as important or interesting to them, they will tend to know and care less about these levels. Some of the public's ignorance of politics, then, may simply be a reflection of our asking them about levels of politics that they care little about. For example, Gus and Gail were two of the three people I talked with who were least knowledgeable about national politics (the third was Nancy). They claimed ignorance about most of the political issues of the day and in a survey would certainly have come across as knowing nothing about politics. Yet both could discuss local politics in some detail, especially Gail. She knew the names of all prominent local political figures and had information and opinions on a number of local issues, while Gus also knew a fair amount about the local political scene.

Conclusions

The scope that people envision for politics underlies the way they make sense of politics. Just as their trust orientation provides a basic orientation toward political leaders and the political system, their scope orientation provides the parameters within which they try to sort out political events. Some make sense of politics by sorting through local issues or the impact of national events and policies on the local community, some by figuring out what is best for the nation as a whole, and others by figuring out the United States' place in the world. People with a local orientation, for example, may decide to support a politician whom they disagree with on national issues if they think that individual is doing a good job of promoting local interests. Someone with a national perspective may support a candidate who they think is a failure in foreign policy if they believe that person offers the best hope for good national policy.

More important than such conscious decisions, however, is that scope orientation affects the kinds of things to which people pay attention. Those with a local orientation are more conversant in local politics than in national politics, those with a national orientation follow national news most closely, and those with an international perspective pay closest attention to foreign affairs. Because of this difference in the scope of concern, people are often ignorant of politics at levels other than the one that concerns them most strongly. Although some people exhibit information about politics at levels other than their main concern (this was most obvious in those with a mixed scope orientation and in those with local orientations resulting from their belief that they could have more influence at the local level), and some people exhibit little knowledge about the level they seem to emphasize (this was particularly true among some of the people with an international perspective), most individuals display variable information levels that seem to be, at least in part, a function of the scope orientation that they possess.

The other important point that emerges from this discussion of how broadly or narrowly people see the political world is that life experiences are very important in helping people make sense of politics. We shall look more closely at the roles of experience, self-interest, and values in Chapter 6, but first we need to look at one other underlying orientation that helps shape people's political perceptions and judgments, the goals that people have for the political system.

5

The ends of politics: Freedom, opportunity, and equality

As I walk through this wicked world, searching for light
in the darkness of sanity, I ask myself, is all hope lost?
Is there only pain and hatred and misery?
And each time I feel like this inside,
there's only one thing I want to know,
What's so funny 'bout peace, love and understanding?

—NICK LOWE

Another orientation that helps to shape the way that people approach politics is their vision of what society should strive for. In one sense there is widespread agreement about the ends of politics. Everyone, or just about everyone, agrees that we should strive for peace, freedom, opportunity, and equality. But this abstract agreement masks some very real differences about what these concepts mean and their relative importance. I will return to a discussion of peace at the end of this chapter, because that goal is discussed most often in regard to international politics. More interesting, and contentious, is the relationship between freedom, opportunity, and equality on the domestic front.

In the abstract, people are quite supportive of all three of these ideals, but in discussions of specific issue areas and the strengths and weaknesses of the United States as a nation, differences emerge in how these ideals are conceived. Jennifer Hochschild's wonderful study of how Americans think about distributive justice, *What's Fair,* shows quite clearly the ambivalences and diffi-

97

culties that people have as they try to make sense of issues of equality and the redistribution of wealth and/or power, as well as the roots and consequences of such beliefs.[1] Here we will look at how these value judgments, once arrived at, help shape the way people make sense of politics.

As Hochschild notes, most Americans see opportunity in terms of equality of opportunity. For them, equality and opportunity are one and the same. Americans may differ as to how much equality or opportunity they view as present in society, but they see no conflict between these goals. My interviewees showed the same pattern. Half of them saw equality and opportunity as compatible goals. However, the other half saw things quite differently. Either they view equality as an end in itself (that is, they favor equal results), or they do not view equality as desirable (that is, they want opportunity to be equal because they believe that the resulting inequalities are a good thing). Additionally, the importance that people place on freedom, and its interaction with equality and opportunity, varies.

Theoretically, innumerable patterns can emerge depending upon the relative weighting of freedom, equality, and opportunity, the extent to which these values are seen as conflicting, and the extent to which these goals are seen as already present in society. But in my sample it was possible to discern four major patterns of values.

The first of these orientations was equality of opportunity. This is the traditional American approach and by far the most common — half of the people I talked to fell into this category. Here, equality and opportunity were viewed as the same thing. Equality was what was needed, but it is seen as equal opportunity. There was no conflict between these values, although there was widespread disagreement on whether the United States offered true equality of opportunity.

Second was egalitarianism. This orientation, held by four of the people I talked with, stressed the importance of equal outcomes. Simple opportunity was not enough. In contrast, the third orientation, individualism, stressed opportunity. What was needed was fairness, giving each individual a chance to succeed, but here there was recognition and approval of the inequalities that resulted from such a struggle. Four individuals had this orientation.

Five people had an orientation I call libertarianism. This orientation was similar in many ways to individualism, stressing opportunities at the expense of equality. However, for each of the individuals in this category, freedom (or liberty) was a much more important factor in its own right. Where the individualists stressed the need for opportunities to get ahead, the libertarians focused on the desire to be free of government constraints. It was the freedom itself that was crucial, not the opportunities that freedom implied. Libertarians also talked about equality in a positive way, because they tended to see equality as equal freedom, not as equal results or equal opportunity.

As with trust and scope orientations, value orientation helps shape the way that people make sense of politics. Their value orientation helps them decide what kinds of things are important, and it shapes the way they approach political issues. They are also likely to judge political figures on whether they seem likely to advance the nation in the appropriate direction.[2]

Equality of opportunity

By far the most common orientation was the one that stressed equality and opportunity as being exactly the same thing. Half of the people I talked to had this approach. Martha Nettles, for example, noted:

> I think one of the great things about America [is] a chance. I think being a citizen of the United States is such a chance to use your talents or just a little bit. You don't even need a whole lot of energy, but just a normal amount of energy. You can get to whatever level. If you don't want to go right to the top, you don't have to try that hard. But if you try a little, if you want to go the first step, then that's all you have to do, and that's what you'll do. But at least you got the chance.

Many of the people I talked with discussed the importance of giving people a chance to get ahead. Opportunities, they stressed, should be available for people. There were, however, large divisions over whether the United States actually provided such equal opportunities. Five individuals—Nancy Gullet, George Heath, Tony Hunter, Laura Rivers, and Gus White—seemed to feel that the United States currently provided real equality of opportunity. George said that the best thing about the United States was "our mobility." Nancy put it this way:

> The life is easier over here than in other places. In this country we have everything. Some people are not satisfied. In the old country, they had to walk half a mile to get a drink of water. Sometimes no lights. They have a kerosene lamp or something like that. They walk barefooted. It's very, very hard in Lebanon some places. But some places it's nice. The rich people are rich, and the poor are very poor. That's what it is, see? This country [the U.S.], they all go downtown. You can't tell the rich from the poor.

Although these five believed that equality (which to them referred to equal opportunities) existed, on occasion they mentioned particular cases of unfair advantage or disadvantage. Gus and George thought that affirmative action quotas were unfair. Gus said: "I'm kind of opposed that government can turn around and say that if you are in business, you have to hire a certain percentage of minorities right away." And George said: "I didn't go for the quotas, though. That ain't right. Quotas. Ten percent should be black. That ain't right. I mean you are hurting white people." Laura expressed displeasure with providing welfare for people who did not work for it: "These people come in, and they can't work or they have children out of wedlock, and they sit back and our money is being given to them that we worked so hard for. . . . I shouldn't think it would be so easy."[3]

But the overall tone of these people's remarks were that most opportunities were equal. There might be a few inequities, but things were relatively fair, so little change was needed in national policy to achieve equality or opportunity. A little tinkering here and there was all that might be required.

In contrast, Al Chambliss, Howard Gossage, John Guidry, and Ed Stanley thought that the country had passed the point of fairness. To them, one of the major problems in the nation was that some people or groups were now being given too much of a chance. Government had gone too far in trying to make things equal and was robbing others of opportunities. John's context was the welfare system: "We have got to have rules in place about going up to the track and betting ten dollars on one horse, somebody on welfare doing that. Then they are crying that they are not getting enough. I think that's one issue that we have to get a lot more stern on. I don't mind paying for people who are less fortunate. But use it to put a clean shirt on someone's back, not to bet ten bucks on the three horse or whatever." Al complained about the effects of affirmative action:

Well, right now, I think, especially a few years ago, [equality has] gone too far. Like what do you call—Jesus, the women and blacks are using it a lot. I forget what it's called. Affirmative action. Now, why should someone be hired if they are not as qualified? I don't think it's right. I just don't think it's right. . . . A lot of it is civil rights. I think you should re-phrase it. I think it should be something like justful equality or something. And a lot of the blacks don't want to be in this place. They'd rather be segregated. Well, if they would rather be that way, and on top of it, if there are problems, because of those two together, maybe they should be segregated. Through choice. I don't want this on the bus, but like in schools. . . . In every city people have to live in the suburbs because they're afraid to send their kids to the city schools because of the violence. Utica's not that bad as far as the things that go on. But kids get hurt, pregnant, they take their lunch money, and all that crap. And it's made the city more of a place of isolation. . . . And that's not good. That's isolation. I think we're creating worse segregation. We really are. I think it's created more of a caste system. "Civil rights" is the terminology. A lawyer must have phrased it. Maybe they just should have said some other word. . . .Maybe it should have been done down South and not so much up here. Equal education. That would have made it. Equal educational rights. Because that's important, and it's a long-term thing. I think people think you can change society in a year or two, and you really can't. But that's tied in to sociology also. People of Italian-American descent, people that, as the generation pro-

gresses, they advance, but you're skipping an important criteria. You take someone out of a ghetto, and four years later he
goes to Hamilton College or some other college, and all of a
sudden he's a professor or whatever the case may be or engineering. He may or may not be qualified, you know, background. It's terrible.

What about the women's rights movement?

I used to go out with a girl years ago when that started, like in
'69. And I think, there again, it should have been equal pay
for equal work. I'll go along with that, even though women
have a higher tendency to be ill and miss work, which is
proven. Which is probably for the children, who are sick
sometimes, or the case may be or emotional or whatever. It's
hard when a wife works full-time. With children it's very
difficult. But in any event, I think it's hurt society.

For these four people, the unfairness they saw was not an
isolated incident or two. It ran to the heart of problems in the
United States today. Equality and opportunity were good things,
but the government had gone much too far. Each of these people
wanted to see major welfare reform, less emphasis on civil rights,
and less government intrusion into matters of equality.

In complete contrast to them were Walter Beattie, Martha Nettles, Ralph Randolph, and Carol Torrez, who thought that equality
of opportunity was the goal but expressed concerns that we had not
gone far enough to reach that goal. Martha, for example, immediately followed her statement about opportunities (quoted above)
with this:

But I wish there were a way—not overnight, I know—but to
have a little bit more distribution of the wealth. There is a lot
of wealth in this country. And I just can never justify in my
mind—there are probably a lot of millionaires, there aren't
that many multimillionaires or billionaires—but in their
whole lifetime they do not need all of that money. Why isn't
there a way to have—somebody says, "Well, there is, if you

are going to work for the state," like whatever, I forget what
you call that. As opposed to a democracy where everyone
works. Capitalism. That's capitalism. Everyone shares, and
there is a more even distribution of wealth. But it absolutely
gets me that some people—and I know some people who are
trying so hard, and five thousand dollars would be like a
million to them—and some people spend five thousand dollars, and they don't even know they are spending it, because
either their financial adviser or something. I find that appall-
ing. That's a problem. Because it starts to—in certain people
anyway, the poor people—after a few years it must really get
them. And they start to get bitter, and I can see why.

Carol noted: "We have made progress, but it is just a sad
situation. There is so much more to be done. And poverty is an
important part of the problem." Ralph said: "There really is not
much for younger kids and older folks. They got nowhere to go
and nothing to do. There are not many jobs at all."

These people, even when they saw problems in terms of inequalities, were concerned primarily with opening up opportunities, making equality of opportunity a reality. Because they thought
we did not have such equality, they recommended that government
do something to change the situation. Walter, Carol, and Martha
thought that providing better educational opportunities was the
key. Walter recommended "equal education to right themselves."
Carol noted we need to do more things like helping people get a
college education: "People complain about the high cost of tuition
in colleges, but one reason it's so high is so many of the good
schools, colleges, want to give scholarships to the deserving poor.
And they do that because they see that the great thing in this
country that has kept it so vital and vigorous is the mobility."
Ralph, on the other hand, talked about the need to provide more
jobs so that people could get ahead. He said our politicians needed
to "build a better future" by creating more jobs.

For these thirteen people, equality of opportunity was the goal
for which society should strive, the value that oriented their vision
of what society should be. Clearly, they perceived great differences
in how much equality existed (in Chapter 6 we will examine the

cause of these differences in perception), and these differences led to different preferences for how policymakers should respond to issues of equality.

Both partisanship and liberal-conservative identification appeared to be linked to people's perceptions of the realities of equal opportunity. Two of the four people who thought we needed more equality (Ralph and Walter) were Democrats; the other two (Martha and Carol) were independents. Similarly, two of those who thought that things were relatively equal (Laura and George) were Democrats, with the others (Tony, Gus, and Nancy) claiming independence. In contrast, of the four people who thought equality had gone too far, two (Al and Ed) were Republicans, and two (Howard and John) were independents.

Of those who thought we needed more equality, Martha, Ralph, and Carol all claimed to be liberal, and Walter called himself a moderate. Two of those who thought things were okay at present had no ideological identification (Gus and Laura), one was conservative (Nancy), and two were moderate (George and Tony). Most striking was that all four of those who thought equality had gone too far were conservative (and all had voted for Ronald Reagan in 1984).

Another interesting relationship was that three of the five individuals who thought things were okay (Tony, Nancy, and Laura) had a supportive trust orientation (they trusted both our leaders and the system). This is the only category of value orientation with more than one individual with a supportive trust orientation. Although I would not want to push a relationship based on so few cases too far, it does seem plausible that people who believe that the system is effectively meeting their political goals would be supportive of the system and the people who run it. Thus, the perception that our country has achieved equality may help lead to a supportive trust orientation.

Despite their different perceptions of how much equality we had achieved, these thirteen people had similar goals for the system. The traditional American image of equal opportunity was at the heart of their thinking. The other people I talked with, however, had a different mix of values.

Individualism

Four individuals—Sue Doyle, Clyde Lyle, Simon Pinella, and Amy Tidrow—had an orientation that I labeled individualism. They were very similar to those with an equality-of-opportunity orientation, particularly those who thought equality had gone too far. These four all agreed that we should strive to give everyone a chance to succeed, but they differed in their perception of what opportunity had to do with equality. For these four people, equality was not really an issue. In fact, they thought there could never be, and should not be, equality. Of the four, Sue had the most complete statement of this perspective:

Realistically, this is the world here, and the nature or whatever. I feel the strong survive. And that's the way it is out in the woods with the animals and the birds. And for some reason today, maybe because of what's been going on and the way people have been thinking lately, somebody wants to have a lot of money and high positions and whatever, but they're not capable. They don't have it, whether it be physically maybe or their capabilities in education, their ability to learn. Maybe they don't have it, to be this big executive and to make a lot of money and whatever. But they still feel as though that job should be there and that they should be doing it. There are jobs out there, and you got to go out and you got to work hard. You got to present yourself. Nothing comes easy. And if you want something, if you want a job that takes a big education, well, some people get their education handed to them. A lot of people have to work for it. If you really want it, you are going to do it. Where there is a will, there is a way. Are you capable, or are you striving for something that you really can't do? And then are you mad after? All right, you got through college, and maybe you didn't have high marks, and it was very difficult for you. But, gee, maybe that isn't something that you were supposed to do. But now you are mad because you sent out three thousand résumés and nobody's hiring you. And people have to be realistic. What are they capable of? Maybe that wasn't what they should have been doing. And they are going to have to settle for a job that pays less money, but they feel that the government, that there should be enough jobs so that I can do what I want. Well, you know, I'm sorry. You are not capable. Or whatever it may be. And they should settle for "Well, maybe this is the only thing I can do." Maybe go find happiness doing something else too. And it isn't up to the government to make sure that everybody has a job that they want.

Amy noted: "There is definitely not equality, and I don't think there will be. And I think that we should just kind of lay off it for a while." Simon put it this way: "I think instead of having special groups with special names, to treat people on their merit . . . to make people stand on their own two feet." And Clyde said: "The marketplace will correct any situations that are unfair."

In these four cases, opportunity was important, not equality. The political consequences of this orientation were similar to those of an equality-of-opportunity orientation coupled with a belief that the government had gone too far. Three of these four (Simon, Clyde, and Sue) were Republicans, and Amy was an independent. Simon and Clyde were conservatives, Sue was a moderate, and Amy a liberal. The three who voted in 1984 all supported Ronald Reagan (Amy did not vote). This individualistic orientation, not surprisingly, seems related to conservative, Republican orientations.

But these people differed from those who thought equality of opportunity had gone too far. Most important, they were much more skeptical of any government policy that sought to promote any kind of equality. The difference in the way they envisioned equality led to a rejection of policies designed to bring it about. They agreed that opportunities should be provided, but they rejected the notion that such opportunities had anything to do with equality. In fact, they opposed the notion of attempting to make things more equal. That, to them, was useless at best and counterproductive at worst.

However, their concern with opportunity allowed them to recommend or support policies that might create opportunities for those who lacked them. As long as these programs were described in the language of opportunity rather than the language of equality, Amy, Sue, Clyde, and Simon were attracted to such efforts. All four talked about improving educational opportunities. Clyde, for example, while discussing the problem of racial prejudice (something he argued was still too prevalent), said: "Giving [blacks] financial aid in terms of going to college and that type of thing would probably help a lot because, you know, you get a degree, you can get a better-paying job." Amy talked about the need to increase teacher salaries to attract better people to the field of education; Sue discussed her satisfaction with New York's state government and her decision to move back to upstate New York because of its good educational system; and Simon commented, "One of the biggest things government could do for the people is reemphasize education."

Three of the four individualists had a skeptical trust orientation; that is, they trusted people but not the system. The exception was Simon, who had a supportive orientation; he trusted people and the system. All four, then, trusted individual leaders to be honest, but three of them thought the system was dangerous. Such an orientation fit with their desire to open up opportunities: Individuals, if given the chance, could be trusted, but when the system interfered with things, by trying to equalize people, for example, the results are harmful.

Thus, the individualists' primary concern was with creating a society that provided people with opportunities. In that, they resemble those with an equality-of-opportunity perspective. But the indiviualists' rejection of the language and concept of equality created differences in the way they approached politics. They often found themselves in agreement with the push for greater opportunities but were quick to pull back when they saw that push turning into a commitment to greater equality, something they saw as unnatural and counterproductive.

Egalitarianism

In complete contrast to the individualists were the egalitarians – Gail Blair, Adam Clay, Mort Johnson, and Ted Munson. Whereas the individualists rejected the notion of equality, the egalitarians embraced it. For them, equality was more than equality of opportunity; some kind of equality in outcome was also desired. For example, while discussing racial matters, Mort said:

> Well, I still think there are parts of the nation where people of different colors are not appreciated, not welcome, looked down upon, and I think we need to overcome all that. Whether they are blacks or whether they are Mexicans or Cubans or whatever, they are still looked down upon. I'm not sure there is equality of opportunity. Well, maybe the opportunity is there, but I am just concerned about the number of street people we have, many of whom are not slouches. . . . It depends on where you want to put your dollars. There is no need for people to live in refrigerator boxes in this nation.

Gail talked about how her daughter could use public assistance:

> I asked her one time, "Why don't you go for a grant?" I says, "You're eligible for a grant." Why don't you try for a grant?" Then I thought she was. And then she didn't, and then she complains. And I say, "Well, it's your fault. Don't complain to me. It's your fault."
>
> *Do you think that there is much that the government can do in that kind of situation?*
>
> I don't see why they shouldn't help. Geez, this is a rich country, this is. It's hard to believe it is. I believe it's a rich country. There is more here than what they say there is. I believe it.

Adam noted: "They should look more toward the poor and middle class and see what they need to better improve them, better improve the lower half of society. I think there is more of an emphasis on what the upper and higher middle class tend to do. I feel more emphasis should be put on the lower middle class and the poor, lower class, because they are not as well off as people with higher incomes, and I feel they should be helped more."

Ted, while discussing how to balance the budget, said: "[We need] to retain the WIC program uncut. I want to see us retain basic, simple welfare." He also talked about redistributing wealth by changing the tax system and using a means test for social security: "Let's take [social security] away from the people who have retired rich and don't need it, and give it to the people who really do."

For these people, a more equal outcome was the goal. Ted and Mort were more supportive of government activity to achieve this goal than were Adam and Gail, whose egalitarianism was tempered by a strong commitment to liberty, which created some skepticism of government programs. But all four saw equality as desirable and as more than simply creating opportunities. They believed that society should ensure that there is much less distance between rich and poor.

The political consequences of this orientation aligned these people with those who had an equality-of-opportunity orientation but thought we needed to go much further to reach that goal. Three of the four egalitarians were Democrats, with Adam being an independent. Ted and Mort called themselves liberal, Adam called himself a moderate, and Gail had no ideological self-identification. Ronald Reagan got no votes in 1984 from this group. They either supported Walter Mondale (Ted and Mort) or stayed home (Adam and Gail).

There were strong differences between this group and those with an equal-opportunity, we-need-to-do-more orientation. An egalitarian orientation created much more concern with the distribution of wealth and power in the nation and much more willingness to support government policies designed to alleviate the problem. All four of these people discussed the need to give the poor more political and economic influence. Ted, for example, noted: "Those groups that don't have the power to motivate themselves with money or with the vote, like the massive group of people that's on welfare, [don't have enough political power]. Underprivileged classes certainly don't have enough power, given the numbers that there are, because I think that money talks. They don't donate to the candidates. For the most part they don't seem to get out there and vote, and so they're somewhat disenfranchised."

In addition, the egalitarians' desire for equality led them to a concern for the rights of welfare recipients. The egalitarians were the only interviewees (except for Laura Rivers) to mention concerns about the way welfare or public-assistance recipients were treated in their programs.

Just as there were many similarities between the individualists and some of those with an equality-of-opportunity orientation, so too were there similarities between the egalitarians and others with an equality-of-opportunity orientation. But in both cases, the difference in orientation also led to important political differences. For the egalitarians, equal opportunity was not enough.

Libertarianism

Five individuals — Mark Dent, Carl Figueroa, Bert Jackson, Dave Thomasson, and Carla Zeber — had an orientation I called libertarianism. For them, the goal of society had little to do with equality or opportunity. Rather, the primary concern was with freedom. Most of the people I talked with expressed a desire to maintain freedom, but what was different about these five was the centrality of that feeling. Their orientation toward politics was shaped much more by their commitment to freedom than by their feelings about equality or opportunity.

For example, when discussing state politics, Carl said: "The seat belt laws, helmet laws as far as motorcyclists, I believe that should be up to the individual themselves. I don't believe you have any right to really stick your nose in there." Bert agreed, noting: "I don't think the federal government should tell me to wear seat belts or tell me that I have to do this here, or they are going to give me that, or they are going to do that. I don't want the federal government funding me any more than I want to fund the federal government."

Carla described what she thought was the best thing about the United States: "It's a free country. You can worship wherever you feel like. You don't have to do what they say. I mean, a certain church, you haven't got to belong to it. . . . [You can] raise your family the way you want to and educate them, and then they can do as they want. The freedom is good." Dave expressed similar sentiments: "Freedom is the first thing. You are not being hammered to go to Oregon or somewheres and look for a place, or any other state of the Union. Where maybe in some other country, you wouldn't have the freedom or that privilege." And, as was noted earlier, Mark voted for the Libertarian presidential candidate in 1976.

For these libertarians, solving problems of equality or creating opportunities was less important than maintaining freedom. Bert, for example, said: "I am not filled with this burning desire to . . . eliminate poverty in America. You realize that by eliminating poverty in America, you increase graft among food distributors eight thousand percent. So you are getting rid of one ill and creating another." Mark was concerned that our freedom was diminishing:

> In my opinion, that's the main thing I worry about, the erosion of rights in the last six or seven or eight years. The police have more power to do whatever they want. I wonder how many people would actually stand up for their rights.
>
> *Can you think of some examples of how our rights have been eroded?*
>
> Well, mostly in criminal ways, the rights of criminals. But the rights of the criminal are the rights of everybody if you are accused of something. And I think that is where it starts.

Politically and in liberal-conservative orientation, this group was quite divided. There were three independents (Bert, Mark, and Carla), one Democrat (Dave), and one Republican (Carl); and there were two conservatives (Carl and Bert), one moderate (Mark), and two with no ideological self-identification (Carla and Dave). Their vote in 1984 was split: three for Ronald Reagan and two for Walter Mondale.

On the other hand, there was a clear relationship between trust orientation and the libertarian orientation. Concern for liberty was linked with distrust of the system and other people. Four of the five libertarians were cynics (they did not trust our leaders or the system). Carla, the exception, was a skeptic (she did not trust the system but trusted leaders). These people believed that political leaders were likely to be corrupt, and the system was corrupt as well, so there was little point in trying to use the system to create equality or opportunities. Rather, the most important thing was to keep that system and those leaders from becoming oppressive. Freedom was the key.

Although these people were skeptical of the government's ability to solve problems, they did not oppose all government ventures. Each of them cited a number of areas where they thought the government could do something to help. But their basic orientation was one of distrust toward these programs, even if they supported the principle of government intervention in some particular area. One such example was Bert's discussion above of what would happen if the government tried to alleviate poverty. Furthermore, when the libertarians did support government activity, they usually justified it as protecting the rights of individuals. When I asked Carl, for example, if he thought the government should be involved in the workplace, he said: "I do. I mean there might be a lot more red tape like [businesses] say and stuff. But I work at X, and we've got machines that put out all kinds of gases and smoke and fumes and this and that, and they're getting away with murder in there. I know they are. . . . [Government] is there to take care of the individual. And you've got to keep the morale of the individual up too."

A just society, for the libertarians, was one that above all else protected individuals and kept people free. Thus, when these individuals looked at politics, freedom was a prime concern. Many of the other people I talked with also were concerned with the maintenance of freedom, but freedom was not as central to their vision of society's goals. Similarly, the libertarians also expressed concerns about equality and opportunity, but such concerns were not as important to them as was freedom. Their value orientation was of a different sort.

Conclusions, and a note about peace

The value orientation of individuals, then, like their scope and trust orientations, helps to shape the way they make sense of politics. Just as an individual's scope orientation affects the level of politics they are concerned with, and their trust orientation affects how they think about the political system and its leaders, their value orientation affects their goals for the system. Their values tend to be a mix of freedom, equality, and opportunity. The relative ranking of these values creates different orientations toward the political world and affects the kinds of policies individuals support and the kinds of problems they think government should address. In addition, for the most common orientation — equality of opportunity — individual perceptions of whether that value has been achieved also are important.[4]

There is also a relationship between value orientation and other political characteristics. Those with egalitarian orientations and with equality-of-opportunity, we-need-to-do-more orientations tend to be liberal and Democratic. Those with individualistic orientations and with equality-of-opportunity, we-have-gone-too-far orientations tend to be conservative and Republican. These coalitions between those with different value orientations, however, often mask important political differences. Egalitarians are much more supportive of government activity than are people who think we need more equality of opportunity, and individualists are much more less supportive of government attempts to help people than are people who think we have gone too far in promoting equal opportunity.

Additionally, there seems to be some relationship between value orientation and trust orientation. People with an equality-of-opportunity orientation who think we have achieved that goal tend to have supportive trust orientations, believing in both the system and its leaders. In contrast, those with a libertarian orientation care little for equality or opportunity but rather are concerned with maintaining freedom, and they tend to be cynical, trusting neither the system or its leaders.

One other important value was expressed, and that was a desire for peace. Every person I talked with said that one of the most important jobs of government was to maintain peace. Here, however, there were differences over whether particular policies will lead to peace. Some, such as John and Carl, clearly supported an approach of peace through strength. Others, such as Dave and Mort, worried about the consequences of a massive arms buildup and therefore expressed opposition to Star Wars (the Strategic Defense Initiative). But no real pattern of orientation toward peace was easy to detect. Everyone voluntarily expressed support for the value, and because we were not directly at war, no one thought that we did not have peace at present. Thus, the differences were over how best to keep peace.

The major line of demarcation was clearly one of how much force was needed to keep peace, but except for a few individuals at either extreme, it was not possible to sort out individuals on such a basis. In Chapter 8, we will look more closely at the individuals with the strongest commitment to using force, because for them, using force was part of a broader stylistic pattern of political thinking that I call macho politics. For most people, the orientation toward peace (with the exception of their support for it) was less stark. They supported peace and negotiations for peace, but they also recognized the need, at times, either to have strong forces or to use force. Few of them talked enough about or knew enough about the details of foreign policy to allow me to adequately characterize where they might fall on a scale that determined their support for the use of force to maintain peace.

Value, scope, and trust orientations, then, are the major underlying factors that emerge as shaping the way that these people make sense of politics. These orientations have a strong impact on the way in which people sort out what is important and what is not. But there is not a one-to-one relationship between these orientations and the particular policies or political leaders that people support, though there are some clear relationships. In order to fully understand the way people make sense of politics, we will now turn to people's sense of fairness, the role that self-interest plays in that conception, and the way that people draw on their life experiences to help them make sense of politics.

6

Self-interest, experience, and politics

Gus White, while discussing OSHA safety rules, said: "They go overboard! Really, I think some of it should be brought down to a more commonsense angle based within the confines of the business concerns."

This expression of a desire for common sense epitomizes one way people attempt to understand politics. In thinking about particular issues or leaders, people look for things that make sense. The question, of course, is, What kinds of things make sense? The answer seems to flow from what I call people's sense of fairness. Common sense is part of this conception of fairness, but before looking at how common sense and fairness interact, we need to examine the relationship between fairness and an individual's material self-interest.

Self-interest and a sense of fairness

The people I talked to all had a sense of what was fair and what was not. This sense of fairness was rooted not in terms of self-interest but in broader conceptions of what is fair.

The role of self-interest in people's views has been studied many times. Despite the appeal of such a concept, there is little evidence to support a large role for self-interest in people's views on politics. Researchers, for example, have found little self-interest in attitudes toward busing, the economy, or public spending.[1] The most careful study of the role of self-interest in taxing issues found only a very limited self-interest effect, one that was much smaller than the effect of symbolic predispositions.[2] My discussions with people yielded similar results. In fact, half (thirteen) of the people I talked with mentioned government policies that they thought should be changed or added even though they knew it would hurt them personally. For example, Ed Stanley discussed a program designed to rebuild apartment buildings in Syracuse, New York:

> Ronald Reagan took office in November and immediately canceled all of Carter's programs, put a freeze on them until he had a chance to review them. And I know there was a class action suit against the U.S. government, because it was already signed into law when it got canceled. They held my application on file for one year. So you can see it cost me a lot of money. But it was a dumb program. It was dumb. I took advantage of it because it was out there. Someone held it out to me and said, "Do you want it?" I said yes. I don't find anything evil with that. It was a dumb program. It cost me a lot of money. I had planned to fix the place up and raise the rents like everybody else was doing. I ended up selling it for just a couple thousand dollars more than I paid for it and not having the quality of tenants that I wanted, so I had headaches dealing with these people for a year. So it cost me a lot of heartaches and a lot of money. But it was a dumb program. I'm glad he got rid of it. And I can sit here and tell you that the American people are better off. I lost, but they're better off. It was dumb.

John Guidry supported a higher drinking age even though it hurt sales in his business, and George Heath supported the Gramm-Rudman budget plan even though it cut his pension's cost-of-living allowance.

Others also were for new policies that they thought would hurt them. Al Chambliss, for example, said: "White flour should be outlawed. We're in the baking industry. We make products for the schools that use white flour, and a lot of that should be outlawed because it's just filled with chlorine. It's okay in your swimming pool . . . [but] it should be outlawed. That's a very important thing." Walter Beattie supported large cuts in defense spending, even though they might have serious consequences for him: "I'm caught in the middle. I work in the defense industry. I work for X, so if there were cutbacks there, I might lose my job."

A few people even expressed a willingness to pay higher taxes in order to solve the deficit problem. Eighty-year-old Carol Torrez described what she thought was the most important problem facing the country: "The deficit, of course. The national debt, and that is all tied in together. I guess that's just about as big as any other. And I would pay more income tax. I would gladly have my social security reduced. I think it is wicked to pay the amount of interest that we are paying on the national debt." Ted Munson said: "I am completely in favor of a tax increase in order to reduce the deficit in order to allow the good social programs to continue."

There were other examples as well. These people were clearly willing to support policies that were not in their self-interest if they thought the policies were in the interest of the nation or were fair.[3]

This is not to say that people did not express self-interest when talking about policies. Martha Nettles, for example, explained how she judges a president: "[By whether I am] any worse off than I was eight years ago, which is probably not a good way to judge it, but that's the way I tend to do it." Clyde Lyle said: "I think tax reform is a good idea because, particularly for me, it's going to be a nice big tax cut."

More important, however, is that people often develop a sense of fairness that is self-interested. That is, their conception of what is fair often will benefit themselves. But it is that conception of fairness, not the benefits, that is the overriding concern, and a conflict between what is fair and what helps them is often decided on the basis of fairness. However, fairness and self-interest often do not conflict. If tax reform is both fair and will help oneself, so much the better. And if one is poor, it is not surprising that one might develop a sense of fairness that incorporates greater help for the needy.

Self-interest is not the only factor that affects people's sense of fairness. The value orientation that people hold also helps shape that sense. People who believe in equality will thus support a greater redistribution of wealth. Of the four egalitarians (those who placed the highest priority on equality of result), only Gail

Blair stood to benefit directly from such a redistribution. The other three egalitarians — Adam Clay, Ted Munson, and Mort Johnson — had little to gain from such a redistribution.

Similarly, it was in the self-interest of some of the libertarians (those who gave the highest priority to maintaining freedom) to support limited government activity in order to maintain freedom and allow the marketplace to provide most of the opportunities, because they had done pretty well in that arena (Carl Figueroa and Bert Jackson, for example). But others, such as Carla Zeber and Mark Dent, probably would have been better off with more government activity.

When we look for the role of self-interest, then, in people's ideas about politics, it is important to remember that its effects can be felt directly (I support this policy because it helps me) or indirectly (I support this policy because it is a good idea that just so happens to help me). From my discussions with these twenty-six people, much more of the latter goes on than the former.

This in turn may help explain why aggregate-level studies seem to find patterns that indicate self-interest among the public even though little such evidence can be found at the individual level.[4] People are more likely than not to hold values and a sense of fairness that are self-interested. When they uphold their views of fairness, they are likely to benefit, at least to some extent. Thus, the rich are more likely to be conservative economically, the poor are more likely to support wealth redistribution, and blacks are more likely to support strong civil rights policies. When we measure aggregate or group differences, we find that blacks are more supportive of the Democratic party, the poor are more Democratic, and the rich are more Republican. Similarly, when things go well, people support the incumbent (he or she has been fair), and when things do not go well, people support the opposition.

But enough people have conceptions of fairness that do not create immediate benefits to themselves that when we try to measure the effect of self-interest on individuals, it is overwhelmed by people's values or political orientations. There are a great many rich Democrats and poor Republicans, and many whites strongly support civil rights. Thus, at the individual level it is much harder to find self-interest at work. Rich egalitarians are more like poor egalitarians in their views than they are like rich individualists.

From my discussions with these twenty-six people, it is clear that when people try to make sense of politics, they do so much more frequently in terms of their sense of fairness than in terms of self-interest. Appeals to self-interest are most effective when they are linked with people's notions of what is fair. People recognize that self-interest (or greed) plays a role in politics, but that is something they dislike. Martha's comment above—that judging a president by how Martha was doing was probably not a good thing—is one such example. Carl Figueroa complained: "There are some that will just go along and couldn't care less. All they care about is what affects their life presently." It is hard to come away from these talks without being impressed by how much people really do try to decipher whether policies and leaders are fair. If what is fair also happens to benefit them, that is fine (and that is often the case), but when a conflict arises, fairness tends to win out.

Common sense and fairness

People develop a sense of fairness that they use to sort out what they like and dislike in politics. This sense is strongly influenced by the underlying orientations that people hold. In particular, their value orientation affects their view of what is fair. But their other orientations also play a role. Trust orientation, for example, affects how they look at the likelihood of the success of a program. Cynics, trusting neither the system nor our leaders, for example, are likely to think that just about any program will be unfair in the end, because rotten individuals and a rotten system will subvert it. Supporters, on the other hand, with their belief in both the system and our leaders, are much more likely to think that programs have the potential to succeed. Similarly, those with a local scope orientation are more likely to focus on a program's fairness to the local community, while those with a national scope orientation will look to the broader effects of the program on the community.

Although these orientations shape people's sense of fairness, people often need more to judge the fairness of a program or a leader. They often rely on what we might call common sense and on their own experiences in life to tell them what is fair and what is not. As I noted in beginning this chapter, people often fall back on common sense when attempting to understand politics.

Probably the clearest example of people's commonsense approach to issues can be seen regarding welfare and welfare reform. I did not ask anyone a specific question about welfare policy, as it was not one of the questions on my master list. Yet eighteen of the people I talked with brought it up as an example of a policy that needed changing or as an example of government waste.[5] They all talked to some extent about the need to make people work for welfare. For example, Carl Figueroa said:

> I don't like the way the welfare system is going. I believe there is a lot of cheating going on there. I believe, again, that should be investigated. I believe at the very least, they should have — I'm relatively middle class, but I get taxed bad. I mean I get hit close to a hundred and fifty dollars' worth of taxes a week. Now, I'm paying for these people, and what are they doing? Sure, they got to go in, they got to sign up, and they go for their classification or whatever it is. Recertification, I guess its called. But the thing is, other than that, they're guaranteed a check, they're guaranteed medical care and stuff, and what do they do for it? I think they should do something for the people that pay the taxes that take care of them. I believe they should have something like back in the thirties. I guess it was Roosevelt, or whoever it is, had these incentive programs. They helped out the people during the thing, but they had to work for the government. I don't care whether you organize these people or they come out shoveling sidewalks, keeping the streets clean, doing things like this. Make these people work for what they get. What right do they have to just sit there and get a paycheck and do nothing for it? And then you got some that are going there, and all they do is have more and more kids because, you know, you get more and more money for it. I mean, what else you got to do? You don't have to work. You don't have to pay anything. I mean, it's more or less taken care of. Your medical. You're getting something for nothing. I don't think its right that me and other Americans have to work, and these people just sit

back, and the first of every month they get a check and don't
have to do nothing for it, except to recertify every so often.

Adam Clay, who had an egalitarian value orientation and displayed a strong commitment to redistributing wealth and power in
the country, said:

> One thing that I never understand . . . is the government is
> supporting all the people on welfare and giving them so much
> money every month or whatever. I feel that they should tell
> these people that you have to work and we will pay you.
> Instead of just giving them money free, they can send them
> out on the streets and clean up the garbage or mow lawns and
> make them earn their money instead of just giving it to them.
> I don't feel it's right that they give it to part of the people and
> not all of the people.

Amy Tidrow felt the same way:

> I realize a lot of people do need [welfare assistance] if they
> are unable to work, or there's not jobs for everyone so that
> everyone is able to work. But I think that there is just no
> motivation after you are on welfare. Really, I don't. I don't
> have any experience in this, but I think that the motivation to
> get a job is lost. There are so many things that these people
> on welfare could be doing. I mean you don't really have to
> give them just the scum-of-the-earth jobs to do, but there is a
> lot of, like, park things that they could do, or not even like
> dollar-an-hour jobs, just things where they could really, really
> earn. It would be more money that they were getting. Even
> though it wasn't directly related to that job—it's from the
> government—but still, I think they should. It would help out
> so much. You wouldn't have to pay these people to do so
> much of this work in the communities and all that stuff.
> Things would get done, and these people would be fed. So I
> think that in exchange for welfare money, there should be
> something that they could do. Either let them pick whatever
> they want to do among so many jobs in the community, or

something like that. But obviously you just can't assign someone to do it, because they won't if they don't like it. But I
think that there should be definitely something to compen-
sate someone for the money that they are getting, including
the people that pay for it, actually. And I think it would give
them motivation too, so I think it would help a lot.

As was noted, eighteen people expressed such sentiments. It
seemed unfair to them that people on welfare should do nothing in
return for the money they receive. And as the sentiments expressed
by Adam and Amy indicated, this was true even for those who
supported welfare policy.

Tax policy was also uniformly seen as unfair. I did ask people
specifically about the new tax legislation, so it was a topic discussed in all of the interviews. Again, an overriding concern was
making taxation more fair. Some people, such as John Guidry,
thought the rich did not pay their fair share: "If I was upper class, I
would think [the tax system] was fair. Okay, I really don't think
your upper-class people should get taxed on the same sense as the
middle- or the lower middle-class people. It seems to be they got
the money, and there's too many loopholes where they can put the
money and no taxation."

Others, such as George Heath, thought that what was needed
was to make the system simpler:

> When you got so many laws, it's tough to do income taxes.
> You are better off doing ten than if you do one, because you
> got to read up on the tax deductions, this deduction, contri-
> butions. And I always thought state tax should be real sim-
> ple, that your state tax could be a percentage of your federal
> tax. I mean, the money would be there. And whatever logic is
> to have federal tax, same logic should apply at the state. And
> at least that would get rid of one piece of paper. And they
> could figure it out easy enough. The federal government
> could tell the state government how much they took in a year
> and figure what our budget was.

Carol Torrez said the system would be fairer if she had to pay
more taxes:

I think New York State taxes are very high. And I can say that because I don't have to pay them on my pension. And neither does Malcolm—what was his name? That former lieutenant governor. . . . I think he has a pension that I read once in the paper—forty thousand. And so those people, big ones who have retired from Albany, are not going to have that law changed. But it would be fairer because if you take all the teachers and all the state employees and so on, if we were paying state income tax also, then other people would be paying less state income tax. So that is just an example of what you might say, unfairness.

People were almost unanimous in finding tax policy to be unfair. But they did not show much consensus over how to make things fairer. Some argued for a redistribution, others for simplification, others for higher taxes for corporations, and still others wanted to cut taxes for everyone. But what was clear was that when people looked at the tax system, they saw something that did not seem fair. The great objection people had to paying taxes was not that they did not want to support the programs they desired, but rather that other people were not paying their fair share. If the people I talked to are representative of the wider public on this issue, the objections to more taxes are more a reaction to the perceived unfairness of the tax laws than to the prospect of having to pay more money. If people could be persuaded that the tax laws were fair, there might be less objection to the prospect of higher taxes to pay for the deficit. But it is hard to imagine that these people would be persuaded that the current system is fair.

Common sense, then, is crucial to people's sense of fairness. Things that do not make sense do not seem fair, and when things strike people as unfair, they object. Two other topics mentioned by a large number of people are good examples of things that did not make sense to them. First was waste in military spending, which was mentioned by sixteen of the people I talked with. Ten of them made specific references to the stories about extremely expensive hammers or ashtrays or coffeepots. These anecdotes about cost overruns for these items stuck with people because they seemed so absurd. It simply did not make any sense to spend, in Martha Nettles' words, "tax money on a hundred-and-forty-nine-dollar hammer." Second, eleven people mentioned the unfairness of spending money on foreign aid when people in the United States needed help.

In other cases, the specific policies that people mentioned varied, but everyone talked about policies that did not make any sense to them, that did not seem fair. Ted Munson talked about the use of the electoral college instead of the popular vote for electing the president. Gus White talked about affirmative action. Martha Nettles talked about subsidies to farmers for not growing crops. Gail Blair talked about the French refusing to allow U.S. planes to fly over their airspace during the bombing raid on Libya. Ralph Randolph talked about raising the drinking age when eighteen-year-olds could still serve in the military. And George Heath talked about supplying arms to both the Israelis and the Arabs. In these and many other cases, different policies were being discussed, but the reasoning of the individuals was basically the same. These policies simply did not make any sense, they did not seem fair, and therefore they should be changed.

When things make sense to people, they are more likely to be seen as fair, but when they are not, they are judged harshly. That, in part, may explain the powerful appeal of Ronald Reagan's claims that government does not work and that taxes and spending should be cut. These ideas appeal to people because they fit within their notions of what is common sense. People have seen examples of the government's not working, people know there are programs that could be cut, and people want to pay less in taxes because other people are already getting away with it. At a basic level, Reagan's claims made sense to a great many people.

Experience and fairness

Another prime source of fairness is the life experiences that people have. In making sense of politics, people find their own experiences can serve as a guide to the broader world of politics. Their experiences play a role by indicating the kinds of policies that do and do not make sense. One of the things I asked people was if there was any waste in government. In response, many of them drew upon incidents of which they had firsthand knowledge or that had been relayed to them by people they knew. For example, Simon Pinella talked about the inefficiency of the government: "They have one person doing one thing and a fantastic amount of vacation. If they're gone for three months, everything sits right there on their desk for three months until they get back. I had instances where I dealt with some of this."

Martha Nettles based her suspicion of government waste on her own experience: "There is probably so much waste. And the reason I'm saying that—I said 'probably'—is that I work for a very large company in this area. It's a very small company compared to statewide or nationwide, but I see the waste. And yet it doesn't seem to be cost-justified to keep a tighter control on it. They say, 'Well, it would cost too much to keep a control on it.' Well, I don't understand that. And maybe that's the way the government feels." Adam Clay said: "I am working for the county on the roads, and I see a lot of wasted money and time in a lot of the things that they do."

Howard Gossage had heard of waste in the school system: "I think the first thing [to save money] is to start with your schools. They waste a lot of stuff. I've been told that by ones who work in the high school." Carla Zeber noted: "I voted against the school budget twice to cut out the waste. Not that I am against them getting books they really need. But I was wondering how much of this they really need. I went to the little country schools, and we didn't have much, and books were high. We had to buy them, so we knew what they were."

These examples and others show that people draw upon their own experiences to help them understand politics. If they hear stories of waste, they take that to be a problem. Argument by anecdote appeals to them if they can relate the anecdote to a similar experience. Perhaps that is why Ronald Reagan's story about the person buying vodka with food stamps (a story with no evidence) was so appealing. People had heard such stories before or had witnessed a similar situation. John Guidry, in discussing welfare, said: "I used to work at the X supermarket. The first of the month, man, the garbage [food stamp recipients] would buy. And I never used to see, in their carts, any kind of soap in them. They used to come in with Pillsbury this. You know there's got to be better control over what the money is being spent for."

People give undue weight to things they can relate to their own life, and thus they end up relying on limited samples to provide them with information about the nation and the world. Al Chambliss, for example, based his notions of what Europeans were like by his interaction with some of his wife's relatives from Germany: "The people [in the U.S.] are much better people. In the nitty-gritty they have bigger hearts, and they're better people." Nancy Gullet and Laura Rivers based their views of the situation in Lebanon on information they had from relatives who lived in that nation. Adam Clay argued that Americans have more freedom than people in other countries: "[In other countries] a lot more things are government-controlled more than I feel like here — it's more free. In Canada, I know, all the liquor stores and stuff like that are all controlled very closely by the government, whereas here, they are generally not controlled as closely."

The problem with limited samples, of course, is that they may not be accurate representations of the whole. Adam, for example, clearly did not realize that laws governing alcohol vary in the United States by state and that there are places in this country with strict state control or even bans on the sale of alcohol. Similarly, Carl Figueroa, who followed international affairs most closely and who thought the United States should have used more force in Vietnam, supported amnesty for those who had avoided service during the Vietnam War: "They evidently saw through the lines like I did. I wasn't drafted, but maybe they were drafted, and maybe they read between the lines, and maybe they had gotten letters from friends saying, 'Hey, it's fricked up over here. This war's being fought screwy.' " Carl did not seem to know that many of those who left the country because of the war did so because they felt the United States was mistaken in the entire venture, not just in the way it carried out that venture.

Experiences, therefore, limit people's visions of political issues and problems, because these experiences affect people's ideas about what is fair. Probably the clearest example of this phenomenon was Sue Doyle's thoughts on what kinds of programs could be cut or eliminated:

Oh, a lot of social programs, so the people would have pride again like in the old days. "No, I don't want to go on welfare,

because I am too proud" and a lot of attitudes like that. Even
our friends that have gone to college, and something happens
to their job — it may not be their fault or whatever — and they
accepted "Well, if I am on unemployment, I get so much a
week." For example, a schoolteacher: "If I go out and sub
every day, make fifty or sixty dollars every day for so many
days, I could make the same amount of money sitting home,
so why should I go out and try and substitute?" Well, how are
you ever going to get another job if you want to get back into
teaching? Subbing, at least you are exposed, and if you are
good, then someone will say, "Hey, we want you the next
opening." But instead they chose to be on unemployment.
And they are not being exposed to their profession and showing their capabilities in some way, and hopefully when an
opportunity is there, they're there.

To Sue, unemployment was a problem of professional people's
refusal to lower themselves, not a problem of the inability of people with no skills or training to find jobs. This conception of the
issue affects her support for major cuts in unemployment compensation.

Sue also commented: "When [a woman] has a baby, nature
intended for that woman to be with the child, and there should be
more mothers at home." When I asked her about women who had
to work to support the baby, we had the following exchange:

Well, that's another story. But we are such a materialistic
world. There's a lot of things that we don't have to have.
There's a lot of women that say they need the second income,
but that's only so they can have more material things. It's
better to give your kid love and attention than giving your
children material things. You can live with a lot less material
things if you had to. . . . I mean, basics, a house to live in,
food, some clothing. You make your own happiness, and if
you think material things can make you happy, well, that's
down the drain. You might as well forget it. It's really the love
you have from your family, your husband — your husband
loves you, and you love him — and your children. And your
happiness, I guess, idealistically should come from people

and not from material things. But in the real world it's another story. I think a lot of women are wound up in the material things, and they are going to work more for material things. And they really could manage with one income. Maybe they couldn't have so many clothes or two cars, but it is hard. It is real hard to stay home and not have money too. It's a vicious cycle. But if the woman chooses to stay home, and the man can't make enough money to put basic food — I don't mean beer and stuff you don't need, but basic food, nutritious food — maybe then those people should be helped until they can.

And for single mothers?

Single mothers, it's rough. Poor things. What do you do? You shouldn't be a single mother.

But sometimes you don't have any choice.

I know. Realistically, what's morally right and realistic, no, I don't know. I guess that's another story. I don't know what the answer is to that. It's unfortunate. It shouldn't happen, but it does happen. I guess in the old days the family more or less took care of the children. And maybe there are so many people that want children too. And if our society wasn't the way it is — because now a woman can do anything. She can have a baby, she can support it, she can go to work, she don't need a man — is wrong because a child does also need a father besides a mother. And maybe if the United States wasn't like it is today, maybe that woman wouldn't have kept her baby. Maybe she would have given it up for adoption. No, this isn't right. A child needs a father. It needs a happy home. And maybe I should give this child up to someone that can give them a happy home, not just material things, but there is a man and a woman. There are so many people that want children that can't have one. And they are dying to have babies. And they would be glad to take this baby and take care of it and love it. . . .There's too many of these single mothers that maybe they should give up their babies to somebody, and then say, "It's not right that I keep this child. How can I give this child what it needs? I can't support it and love it and be there and go out and work." Nature intended at least two people to bring up a child.

Sue simply could not see the problems that poor people in general and poor women in particular faced. The thought that a single mother might be someone who was divorced and left with young children was not something she could easily imagine. Her solution, that single mothers should give up their children, was not one that most single mothers would endorse. But Sue's views of politics were limited by her experiences, and this phenomenon was at work to some extent in all of the people I spoke with.

Experience and political orientation

The experiences people have help to shape not only their views of specific issues and their sense of fairness but also the basic orientations discussed in Chapters 3 through 5. Although it is not always possible to trace how experiences shape those basic orientations, it is clear that such a relationship exists.

In this study, trust orientation was often a function of people's dealings with the government and with other people. Gus White related his distrust of politicians to his own experience as an officer in his fraternal organization:

These guys were down there one time really rubbing elbows with you, being friendly and smiley, smiley. Now all of a sudden they are so far above that it's like so high up looking at ants, and they're controlling it. They're controlling their movements and their lifestyles or having something to do with it. And that echelon of power, all of a sudden they get to a point, they really escape the everyday realities of real living, down-to-earth nitty-gritty survival. . . . Would my principles and my beliefs and my morals be the same if I turned around and jumped up these levels where all of a sudden I am power? I can turn around and talk about, shit, I don't know what the hell it is on a political level, but just joining a local fraternal organization, the difference between being just a member and going into, say, an officer, of the fraternal organization, but then jump from there into, say, a division of half-a-dozen of the fraternal organization, within it, and become the president of that. I know what that's like. And believe me, it is amazing, and that's just a little bit of a level for me. And I'm a snot by nature, right? Or by comparison. So I can just imagine what like all these politicians are jumping into.

When he compared the power of politics to his own reactions to power, Gus became distrustful. Similarly, Laura Rivers related her trust of both the system and leaders (a supportive orientation) to the fact that "on the whole, I think life is pretty good — I'm happy." Martha Nettles' supportive orientation was linked to her strong religious beliefs.

The other strongly religious individual was Dave Thomasson, but in complete contrast to Martha, he was a cynic (trusting neither leaders nor the system). This orientation also came from his experiences. He told me: "I lived a bad life myself. I was born. I had nothing to do with who I was. I became an altar boy. Then I became a choir boy. And then when I grew up, I became a bad boy, gambling, drinking." Although he later rediscovered religion, and that religion was important in helping him think about politics (Dave often discussed political issues with religious analogies from the Bible), his earlier period of problems left him distrustful of people and concerned with the ability of power and money to corrupt the system.

Sue Doyle's skepticism (her distrust of the system combined with trust of leaders) developed when her husband worked for the federal government, and she saw how the system could corrupt people. Mark Dent's cynicism evolved from his experiences in Vietnam. The extreme example of how our experiences shape our level of trust in other individuals and the system was Bert Jackson, whose cynicism had developed to the point that he did not trust anything that was not within his own experience. Near the beginning of our conversation, he said: "I never got a chance to one-on-one with Ronald Reagan. I think that what happens in this country, a lot of people become cynical because you can feed them baloney twice, and after a while everything they eat tastes like baloney to them." Toward the end of our almost four-hour-long session, he said:

> You want me to cap this whole thing for you? The worst thing
> about politics is the fact that no one knows anything about
> politics enough to give you an accurate description of what's
> wrong with the system. I don't even know how the system
> works, if you ask me that. I don't even know anything about
> politicians other than what I am told. They might not even
> exist. I see them. That's not good enough. I don't know
> Ronald Reagan. I don't know Jimmy Carter. I don't know
> Mario Cuomo.

Bert trusted only what he experienced firsthand, and those experiences had made him very cynical.

Just as trust orientation is shaped by life experiences, so are people's scope and value orientations. In Chapter 4 I discussed the link between life experiences and scope orientation. We saw how education tends to broaden one's scope, how religion seems to lead to a global perspective, and other examples of this relationship. Carl Figueroa had developed an international scope as a result of his fascination with the Vietnam War, and Ted Munson, Al Chambliss, and Ed Stanley had developed a local orientation because their experiences with local politics had led them to believe they could have more influence and were more affected by local events.

In a similar way, value orientations also rise from life experiences. Simon Pinella developed an individualistic orientation (giving the highest priority to opening up opportunities with little or no concern for equality in outcome) as a result of his own success in working his way up through the system: "I deal with a lot of people who complain they want more programs, more help. But I come from a low income and rose to a higher-middle-income group through hard work." Sue Doyle's individualistic orientation developed from her successful career (before leaving work to have a child) and her observations that some people had the talent to succeed and others did not.

In contrast, Ted Munson's egalitarian value orientation (giving priority to equal outcomes) were shaped while he was a college student in the late sixties. Gail Blair's egalitarianism developed out of her own poverty and struggle to make ends meet in spite of doing all she could to succeed.

Within the dominant equality-of-opportunity orientation (which sees equality and opportunity as the same thing), perceptions were a product of people's experiences. Those who thought equality had gone too far — Ed Stanley, Al Chambliss, John Guidry, and Howard Gossage — all told anecdotes about how they knew or had seen people taking advantage of the system. They thought these people should not be given so much help. However, the four people who thought we had further to go to achieve equal opportunity — Walter Beattie, Martha Nettles, Ralph Randolph, and Carol Torrez — all knew people who needed more help.

Government performance, political style, and experience

Clearly, then, as people attempt to understand politics, they draw upon their own experiences. Their basic orientations and their thinking about specific issues are shaped by their lives. Perhaps most significant is that their experiences tell them what is important.

In thinking about politics, people are faced with a practically endless set of issues, problems, and solutions, and making sense of it all is difficult. Relying on experience is helpful but can be limiting. People do not know from their own experience how to balance the nation's budget (though many of the interviewees knew it was important to balance a budget because they knew what happened to people who lived beyond their means), nor do they know how much defense capability the nation needs, nor do they know how to solve social problems (though their experiences tell them what kinds of solutions make sense). But there are two areas where people have confidence that their experiences can provide the necessary information — government performance and effective political style.

A number of the people I talked with cited performance as one of the factors they use to judge government officials.[6] To some extent, the kinds of anecdotal evidence we looked at above are performance judgments.[7] People see things going wrong with the system, and they judge it harshly. If they see people getting away with cheating on welfare or food stamps, as Al Chambliss, Ed Stanley, Bert Jackson, John Guidry, and others claimed to have seen, then those programs must be faulty. If they see the criminal justice system treating people unfairly, as Ralph Randolph and Ed Stanley claim, then there must be a problem.

Performance judgments, however, can also be broader. Walter Beattie mentioned Mario Cuomo: "He had a budget in the black the last few years, and he gave most of us a tax break." George Heath said he judged candidates by "past performance, by how the economy is doing." Laura Rivers compared Carter and Reagan by citing the cost of groceries during their administrations.

It is much easier for people to use their experiences to get a handle on how things are going than it is to judge what will happen in the future. Still, come election time, people also like to make evaluations of which candidate is likely to do better. Past performance can help here, but another factor people often draw upon is political style. We saw in Chapter 2 that some people seem to think about politics more in terms of styles than in terms of policies. One reason for this is that styles can be related to people's own experiences.

Ed Stanley, in discussing the need for an arms buildup and a tough president, said: "I know how many times I got punched in the mouth when I was in high school and how many times people smaller than me got punched in the mouth. And it's kind of strange. We could be sitting right next to each other. But someone would pick on them and not me. And I wasn't necessarily a part of the bully's crowd either."

Tony Hunter described the importance of listening:

> I think a good politician's got to listen. He's got to be a good listener before he can be a good talker. I learned that the hard way. When I first started working, I went in with the attitude, well, I knew it all. And I found out quickly I didn't know any of it. So I reversed my whole attitude, and I listened. And I listened and I listened and I listened before I spoke. And it helped me in the long run. And that's what I try and instill in my kids. And my wife tries to instill in me, still. But I think a good politician will listen.

Sue Doyle thought that taking responsibility was important:

Like President Reagan says, the buck stops here. And that's right. Whenever you are leading something and you are in charge, you know you get your advice from all the people around you, and the people who are around you are ones you pick, and hopefully you pick the person for the job not because you owe them it. But you are the one that has to make the final decision, and you are the one that is responsible. That's what I believe. For all the organizations that I am in, when I am in charge and I have responsibility, I feel that I am responsible for it, so therefore the buck stops here. It's important to be strong and listen to everybody's opinion, but you have to come out and make the decision. You are responsible for it. He does take responsibility for what goes on. And I think it makes it seem, he's much stronger. He seems to be much stronger a man. And then the other countries look at us as a stronger country whenever, I think, the president seems to be a strong leader.

George Heath did not like Ted Kennedy: "Because of Chappaquiddick. I think that was a sign of weakness. Going home to mama there to see what he should do about the accident. Man, that's scary. What if he's president and the bomb comes? Are you going to ask your mother what to do?"

Dave Thomasson commented:

[The nation's leaders should] take a good look in the mirror and see what you are doing to improve not only your personal life but the life of your neighbors, the life of your townspeople. What are you contributing to what you are criticizing? . . . For me, I just try to live each day as being fair and square with my neighbor, with people I meet whether I know them or not. If someone needs it, I try to help. I find that's what I live for. My lawn mower just busted, and today I was trying to push it around, and my neighbor came over and says, "Put that away, and come over and use mine."

People can look around themselves and see what kinds of people succeed and what kinds fail. They see what kinds of people do good things and what kinds do bad. And they try to get a fix on what kind of people our political leaders are. As the above examples show, however, people look for different styles. This concern with style is aided by the media, which find it easier to focus on personality than policy. Television is much better at portraying the human side of a story—the side that focuses in on the people and what they are like—than it is at portraying complex policy problems. That is why television docudramas and movies that look at social issues usually tell a story via portraits of people. This in turn fits with the easier time people have making stylistic judgments about political leaders than judging policy positions.

Style becomes a way for people to measure future performance. They can see, through their own experiences, that people with particular qualities are likely to succeed, and they look for those qualities in their leaders. Their experience may not tell them whether Ronald Reagan or Walter Mondale has a better plan to solve the problem of the deficit or drugs or relations with the Soviet Union, but their experiences can tell them which person has a style better suited to lead the nation or solve those problems. It is not a matter of style versus substance. Rather, style is a way to get a handle on substance. People do make judgments about issues and policies; some people, in fact, rely primarily on such factors when evaluating candidates. But the experiences that people draw on to help them make sense of politics often leave them better equipped to judge style than to evaluate policy.

Conclusions

People's experiences have a variety of effects on how people make sense of politics. First, experiences help shape the basic orientations that underlie people's thoughts about politics. Trust, scope, and value orientations, which provide the context in which people think about policies and political leaders, are all shaped, at least in part, by people's experiences.

Second, the experiences that people have help shape their views of political styles that are likely to succeed. Their experiences also allow people to make judgments about whether a particular policy has succeeded or failed. They prefer to use firsthand experience to judge government performance.

Additionally, people's experiences help shape their view of common sense, and their sense of fairness. People learn, through their lives, what kinds of things make sense and what kinds do not. This in turn helps them decide what kinds of policies are fair and what kinds are illogical. (The sense of fairness also evolves from the underlying political orientations that people have, particularly their value orientation.)

Experience can also help people make judgments about particular issues. However, in this case, the limitations of relying on a small sample for information can create difficulties in sorting out the complexities of political issues. (A number of the people I talked to, for example, stated that they did not have an opinion about a particular issue or program because they had no experience with it.) This is one reason why people may rely on style judgments rather than policy judgments to make sense of politics. They are better equipped to relate their experiences to style evaluations than to policy evaluations.

In thinking about issues, people use their experiences to help formulate their sense of what is correct, and they also rely on fairness. People try to move beyond their own self-interest in judging policy matters and instead try to make decisions based on broader conceptions of fairness. (These conceptions come not only from people's experiences but also from the underlying political orientations that they hold.) Still, partly because of the limiting nature of most the experiences that people have, people's conceptions of fairness are often self-interested. What's fair is often what is good for the individual. However, when what's fair conflicts with what's good, what's fair seems to win out most of the time, though there may not be many cases in which these conflicts arise.

In Chapter 8, we will return to the issues of style, policy, and making sense of politics as we put together the various patterns of political thinking. But before doing that, we need to look at the inconsistencies and ambiguities that are present in the way people think about politics and how people deal with them. As we shall see, the ambiguities of politics are another force that drives people to prefer to make sense of politics in terms of style rather than policy evaluations.

7

Ambiguity
and confusion
in politics

In exploring how people make sense of politics, we have concentrated on the underlying orientations and ideas that people have. This may give the impression that it is relatively easy for people to sort out what goes on in the political world. In looking at the ideas that people have, we have thus far neglected the difficulties and problems that people have in figuring out what goes on or where they stand on a particular issue. In this chapter, we will examine those difficulties and problems. We will begin by looking at people's attitudes toward democracy and democratic procedures and then move to a broader discussion of how people cope with uncertainty in politics.

Attititudes toward democracy

One of the clear findings of survey research, is that people have ambiguous attitudes toward democracy. People support democratic principles in the abstract but are often willing to sacrifice those principles in concrete situations.[1] In this study I did not pose specific questions about the application of democratic principles, but some of the ambiguity and confusion about democracy was evident in the discussions that I had.

All twenty-six of the people I spoke with expressed support for the principles of democracy, but not all were happy with some of the consequences of democracy. Probably the clearest (or at least the most self-conscious) example of this dichotomy was Bert Jackson, who constantly expressed support for democratic principles. He said the job of a member of congress was "to represent the majority of his people" and that "when they start making laws that affect a minority and disallow what the majority feel, something is wrong." Bert complained strongly that an area representative had voted for a tax increase even though his constituents opposed it. But in discussing the need for educational reform, he said:

> They had this restructuring proposal in Utica. The politics involved in it. They said, "Hey, let's do this. We will get this guy to come in and evaluate the whole system, as you read in the papers, and we will see what the average people think on the streets." That's a mistake, because the average people on the street don't know what it takes to educate people. You shouldn't leave that decision with people, because invariably you are going to get a bunch of responses that are going to be directed toward monetary considerations, local considerations, not that the overall aim of the project, which is to make a better overall education within a limited budget, see. So when I say the government should streamline itself and pay more attention to the people, what I mean by "the people" is what I mean by what we consider should be done. If we think crime is okay and everybody should be snorting cocaine, and if the people think that and the government obviously doesn't think that, well, I am not telling the government to do it because the people want it. I am sure that is not the case. But what I am trying to say is, I don't want you to come across with the impression that I think they should be responsible to every whim and whimsical drive of the people.

Bert thought leaders should listen to what the people wanted, but not on every issue, because on some issues the people did not know what was correct.

Al Chambliss argued that one of the good things about the country was the influence that citizens had and that they should use it even more than they did. He said that "politicians are very vulnerable, and we don't take advantage of that" and that this

potential vulnerablity was "fantastic." On the other hand, he argued: "Politicians, as you know, are always so afraid of making
changes. They want to get reelected. It's unfortunate. They should
have a four-year term or whatever it might be as governor, a six-
year term, and not be able to be reelected." To Al, it was good that
politicians were vulnerable, but the cause of that vulnerability,
their desire for reelection, could make them act improperly.

Ambiguity about the results of some of the things that people
like about our democratic system was present in most of the interviews. Ed Stanley, for example, expressed support for majority rule
but then worried about the role of welfare recipients in New York
State elections:

> Perhaps the day before the election, the governor will come
> on and allude to the fact that his opponent . . . was going to
> cut their checks. I'm not saying welfare people shouldn't have
> the right to vote for governor, but I feel if the issue is their
> check and their benefits which come out of our tax dollars, I
> feel that somehow they should be affected. I've already stated
> I am not against welfare. I would like to see the law return to
> take one [cheating] welfare recipient and get rid of her and
> add ten to the list. I'd rather pay ten dollars to have some-
> thing good than a dollar for nothing, because one is waste
> and the other is not. I don't know if the rest of the taxpaying
> public feels the way I do, but I do believe in majority rule. I
> do believe that [taxpayers] are the ones affected in their lives,
> though the welfare people are too. I just would like to see the
> taxpayers have more say in what is going to happen to them.

Howard Gossage told me that the best thing about the United
States was the freedom: "If you want to work, [you can] find a job
that you want." On the other hand, he said: "If [welfare recipients]
came up from the southern states, send them right back there. Why
should they come up and live off us?"

Carl Figueroa also had some ambiguity regarding freedom.
He said: "Freedom is what this country is about, freedom of
speech, the freedom to say what you think." But he had this to say
about the Vietnam era:

If you're going to wave Vietcong flags, that's when they should have let the police out or the hard hats or whoever. I guess there was that clash between the hard hats and the peace demonstrators. Let the hard hats out, and let them do a number on these people, because these people are communists or traitors, and I have no respect whatsoever for these kinds of people. But if you want to march and you want to protest and you want to have your sit-down strikes, that's fine. You want to carry your placards, fine. But no Ho Chi Minh. That's a bunch of bull. You're a traitor then. Because then you're rooting for the enemy.

Adam Clay believed that members of Congress should do what they could for their districts: "He should say, 'I'm going to fix this town, this road.' He should be a lot more specific with the needs of the people." On the other hand, Adam said: "One type of thing that goes on that I personally don't like is, the congressman wants to get a bill through for his area, [so] he makes deals with all these other congressmen. You want some of these things, I'll vote for you. One hand washes the other. That type of policy, to me it doesn't fit. I know it goes on all the time. . . . But to me it just tends to hurt everything more than help anything."

As a final example, Carla Zeber expressed concern that the president is often slowed down by Congress and thus "is only allowed to do so much." But when I asked her if it would be better if we changed the system to speed things up, she said: "It depends on the issue. If the issue was a good one, it would be good to move fast. But if you weren't certain for sure, it's good that it has to wait."

People tended to support democratic ideals and principles and endorse our system, but sometimes the results of that system or the implementation of those ideals made them leery. The results did not strike them as fair, and they wondered how the system might be changed or interpreted to lead to a better result. At times this ambiguity was conscious, as in the case of Carla, who thought a change would help on some issues but hurt on others, or Bert, who recognized his seeming contradiction in supporting majority rule but also believing there were issues that should not be left up to the people. In most cases, however, people did not recognize the ambiguities they voiced, or as in Carl's case, they were able to distinguish between a proper and an improper use of democratic principles. Furthermore, confusion or ambivalence about politics was not limited to issues of democracy and the functioning of our political system.

The complexity of politics

Everyone I spoke with expressed confusion or concern about some of the issues they saw facing the nation. Some of these concerns took the form of the kind of dichotomy just discussed between principles on the one hand and results on the other, but in other cases it was a simpler confusion over how to deal with specific issues. On the issue of abortion, Amy Tidrow said:

I have thought and thought of the situation, and I can't come up with an answer. I mean, I don't like to think, "Yes, I am for it. Yes, I am against it. Yes, I think they should give aid. No, I don't. Yes, it should be legal. No, it shouldn't." I mean, there are just so many situations that I can think of that people would be in or why they should spend money or why they definitely should not, why it should be legal, why it should not. I just can't come up with a yes or no answer to that. . . . The thing is, I can't make a decision that if someone said, "Well, what about this and this?" and I say, "Yeah, maybe I am not against it" or "Yeah, maybe I am not for it." There are just too many things, emotional things and legal things and so many things involved that there is just no way. I don't know if I ever will. Hopefully I will be able to, because it would be nice to just say yes or no. But there are just too many things involved that I can't really make a decision yes or no as far as political. So I don't have much of an answer on that one.

Walter Beattie said that the most important political problem facing the nation was the budget deficit. But when I asked him if he had any idea what could be done about it, he said: "Well, I haven't given it much thought. I leave that to the politicians. But I would think raising taxes would be one thing. . . . Of course, when you raise taxes, I do believe that you hurt the economy, and so if you hurt the economy, you don't have the revenue. . . . It's a difficult situation. They have got themselves into a box, and it's not easy to get out." When I asked Bert Jackson about the deficit, he said: "What does the deficit mean? My friends who are economists, they can't tell me what it means either. So I am not even going to touch that question." Nancy Gullet said: "I heard lots about this deficit. Every time I open the television, I hear that. But I don't know what it is."

The trade deficit also created confusion. Mort Johnson said: "Well, I think our balance of trade is all screwed up. Probably something is going to have to be done about that. But I don't know what the solution is." Laura Rivers noted: "Imports are a problem. . . . But I wish I knew more about importing and exporting. . . . I really shouldn't comment."

Mark Dent found the social problems of crime and drug abuse difficult to deal with. He commented: "There aren't any simple solutions to all those things, so it's easy to say that the government isn't doing enough or is not doing a good job. But there aren't any alternatives that make sense for most of these issues." John Guidry thought that government waste was a major problem, but he also said, "I don't know if much could be done, but something better be done." Gail Blair considered unemployment to be a major issue, but when I asked her what she thought could be done about it, she said she didn't know.

The issues that elicited the most confusion and ambiguity were those of foreign policy. Carol Torrez discussed the issue of arms and negotiations: "Weaponry has become, like everything else, so expensive. We have to have some. But I do think that they realize now that we have to be more careful about the costs. . . . But it's a big problem. I think it is more of a man's problem. And it certainly isn't a problem for an old lady. But it bothers me. It worries me. How much should we spend? Is that the way to prevent a nuclear war?"

Laura Rivers commented on Central America: "That's another one. Contra. I don't know what Contra is. No, I haven't followed that too much, other than rebels and guerrillas and President

Reagan is trying to—is he promising them aid? I think it went through, but I really haven't followed that." George Heath said:

> You know, I can't keep score down there. I think what the Contras are for, and then in the other country next door— Honduras, isn't it? Nicaragua and Honduras. We're support there, there is intermix, and now the Panamanians are getting in the action. Jesus. Then, maybe, I justify myself for not knowing all the details for all this—even though I have access to magazines, papers—because knowing, you can't do much. I know you can vote. But it gets frustrating, even if it could affect you, if you are a sensitive person. Some people maybe shouldn't even read the front page.

And Martha Nettles had this to say about Central America: "I get very mixed up with the countries and the names, and a lot of times I'll ask my second son or my third son, 'What is going on here? Why does the president want to give money to the Contras? Is that right, the Contras?' And the word *Shiites* comes into it. 'That's a different country,' my son will say. And I get very mixed up." Simon Pinella noted that Central America was "one of the neglected areas that I don't know very much about."

Over and over again, on a wide variety of issues, people talked about not understanding or not knowing what to do. They often thought something was wrong or knew there was a problem, but they did not know what should be done or how to decide if current policy was correct. Dealing with such issues created a good deal of confusion or ambiguity among the people I spoke with.

The causes of uncertainty

In the examples cited above, people gave a variety of reasons for their uncertainty. Probably the most common was the complexity of the issues. Amy's thoughts on abortion, Walter's comments of the deficit, and Mark's views on crime and drug abuse were examples of this. In each case the problem was recognized as having no simple solution, and, consequently, there was a good deal of uncertainty about what to do.

The examples of ambiguity over democracy and democratic principles pointed to a second cause of uncertainty: People often had conflicting goals. In the case of democracy, people often found that their support of democratic principles led to undesirable results. For example, if welfare recipients vote to raise taxes the goal of democracy conflicts with the goal of lower taxes. When Carl commented on the Vietnam War protesters, his belief in freedom conflicted with his goal of fighting communism. When we have multiple goals for society, and we all do, it is hard to balance the conflicts that can arise in implementing these goals. Another example of this was seen in Sue Doyle's discussion of what to do about the problem of chemical additives in food. As was noted earlier, Sue believed in very limited government. But she also said: "The food industry is really ripping us off. Paying big bucks for all this food, and a lot of it, there is not even any food in it. It's all chemicals." It was not clear to her what could be done about it:

> I don't know if it's the government. It really isn't the government. Well, government controls the food industry. Maybe I guess it is. Maybe the government should do more about it. Rules and regulations saying we shouldn't be feeding our people this kind of stuff. We should be eating more real food and not worry so much about making the big bucks. But then, let's be realistic. Oh, I don't know. I can't say who should be doing this, doing that, all the pros and cons of everything.

Thus, the problems of complexity and conflicting goals often led to uncertainty and confusion. But there were also more personal causes of uncertainty. First was that people felt overwhelmed with information. They just could not keep up with all that was going on. George's and Laura's discussions of Central America were two examples of this. Dave Thomasson discussed this problem in a more general way: "I follow [politics]. I read quite a bit of the papers, almost from one end to the other. There is so much contradictory stuff in there that you don't know which end to believe, which way it is going." There is so much information, and it is so often contradictory, that people feel incapable of keeping up with it, especially since, as we saw in the first chapter, politics is not a high priority for most people.

Closely allied with this was a second personal cause of uncertainty: feelings of personal inadequacy. Sometimes people thought the fault was their own. They did not understand enough. Laura's confession that she should know more about importing or exporting, and Martha's discussion of Central America fell into this category, as did Gus White's comment that he didn't "follow politics in a real deep critical sense."

Thus, both the nature of the issues (their complexity and the conflicts of goals) and the way people relate to politics (its relative low priority coupled with massive amounts of information and, at times, feelings of personal inadequacy) lead to confusion and ambiguity about politics. This confusion in turn leads to a variety of responses.

How people deal with uncertainty

People respond in a variety of ways to the uncertainty they feel about the political issues and problems that they see. One factor that seems important in determining their response is trust orientation. Cynics, who lacked faith in both the system and our leaders, tended to respond with feelings of alienation and frustration. Gus White, Howard Gossage, Dave Thomasson, and Gail Blair all talked about their despair over what could be done to solve some of these problems, and their distrust of the political system to do anything about them. Bert Jackson had some of these feelings, particularly the distrust of finding any real solutions, but he was not as completely turned off by the system as the other four. Of the seven cynics, only Carl Figueroa and Mark Dent seemed to avoid this feeling of almost complete alienation. That feeling of alienation was largely limited to the cynics. Of the other people I talked with, only George Heath showed any strong feelings in that direction. His comments about Central America were a good example of this.

At the other end of the spectrum were the supporters, with faith in both the system and our leaders. Their response was often one of trusting our political leaders to do what was best. Martha Nettles, after noting her confusion about Central America, said: "Again, my trust in Reagan. I just feel if he thinks this is the thing to do, then he certainly has all kinds of advisers, and he's intelligent enough himself to know to make a decision. And if this is his decision, boy, I'm with him. Boy, if he thinks we should still be helping this group of people, whichever group of people it is now who are in power or not, I'm for it."

Laura Rivers, Nancy Gullet, and to a lesser extent Simon Pinella and John Guidry displayed similar reactions.[2] If they were confused by a policy or problem, their tendency was to support what our leaders recommended. However, they did not agree with all government policies in all areas. Rather, for issues that they felt unknowledgeable about or that they didn't have answers for, they were likely to give our leaders the benefit of the doubt. For issues that they were more certain about, they were all willing to find fault with current policy. (However, two of the supporters—Tony Hunter and Adam Clay—did not seem to exhibit this tendency of giving support if they were unsure about the issue.)

Only one individual who was not a supporter had this response to uncertainty: Sue Doyle. Although Sue was skeptical of any domestic government activity, she was willing to trust government officials on foreign-policy issues when she did not know how to solve a problem or was confused:

> We are trying to fight communism in all these countries, and all these wars are breaking out, and I'm sure that we are causing some of them, you know, having our people in. For some reason we want this leader to lead the country. Whatever reason, I don't know. All the little countries in South America or wherever. And the revolt. And I know that we support them or whatever. And I know that the government came out and said, "No, we are not doing anything in this country." But you know, you look at the Vietnam War and the war in Cambodia, and all those countries. We were there anyway. But what do I know about all this stuff? They are keeping it secret for a reason. They feel as though maybe this one leader should lead this country, and the other one shouldn't, because this one will favor us and not communism. And you read in the paper, it's really not what's really going on. Maybe that's why I just don't bother. They're not telling us everything. And I don't think that they should.

What's the security of our government if everybody goes and blabbers what our secrets are? Tell us, well, we are starting this war over here and this revolution. We want this guy, but it's going to be better for this country because the other guy is a communist. I am not going to argue. What do I know? And so I don't bother to keep up with that. And I am sure that maybe there are times when we shouldn't have done what we did. But we are doing what we can do. It's very difficult to fight communism peacefully. And when they come over, and they are aggressive, and they do things that they shouldn't do, and it's hard to always be right and never be wrong. And we tried to do that. And I'm sure there are times when we shouldn't have been places where we were. . . . And there is probably a lot of things that I wouldn't like and all, but if I don't know about them, then I don't have to worry about them neither.

As this statement indicates, Sue was skeptical that our leaders always did the right thing. Sue was quite willing to offer her views on what we should be doing differently with domestic policies, but in foreign affairs it was easier to deal with her uncertainty by trusting our leaders to look out for our best interests. Like most of the supporters, the skeptical Sue was willing to defer to authority in some areas where she felt unknowledgeable. Because people are more likely to feel uncertain about foreign policy than domestic policy, there is a greater cushion of support for government officials in foreign affairs. People's confusion or lack of information causes them to be more trusting of foreign policy.

Still, most people do not react with either complete trust or complete alienation. Rather, most people feel some kind of need to make sense of the issue at hand, but because that is often difficult, people respond by falling back on the things that they do know. They try to think about issues in terms of the values and orientations that they have. For example, after telling me that he did not know what we should do in the Middle East because it was so complicated and we had so many different interests involving energy resources, Simon Pinella said: "Maybe we should be more strict than we've been, because of just the pride you have in America."

Rather than deal with the complexities of the issue, it was easier for him to turn the issue into one of American pride and deal with it that way. Thus, it is sometimes possible to transform a complex issue into an issue of which some sense can be made. Issues of foreign policy can become issues of American pride. The federal deficit can become a simple matter of living within our means, without reference to the choices that have to be made. The problem of what to do about welfare can become one of eliminating fraud and deception. These are "simple" ways to comprehend complex issues and are therefore attractive to people who are bewildered by political complexities. But even this approach is often difficult because people recognize the complexity behind the simple issue. They know that eliminating waste will help, so they support it, but they also recognize that solving problems of poverty is not easy. The kind of commonsense approach we saw in the last chapter becomes helpful here, but what complexity seems to do most of the time is to drive people away from trying to understand politics in terms of issues.

Many of the people I talked with tried to understand politics not by making sense of issues but by making sense of styles of politics. That is, rather than deal with how to solve a particular problem, they looked for people who would approach the problem in a way that they thought could solve it. Being tough or being compassionate can be the solution to the welfare problem in the sense that the style with which the problem is attacked will lead to the proper kind of solution. One does not need to get into the overwhelming specifics of how to solve the problem, but one can make sense of how to approach the problem.

Just as important is that people can make sense of styles from their own experiences. They may not know how to solve the problems of welfare or crime or war in Central America, but people know, or think they know, that being tough (or compassionate or open-minded or generous) will or will not be likely to lead to solutions. The people I talked with preferred to trust their own experiences to help them make sense of politics. It was easier for them to find examples of styles that would or would not work, and to think about politics that way, than to find examples of how to deal with specific policy issues.

Thus, the ambiguity and complexity that individuals see when they try to understand political issues that are important to them often lead them to try another approach. If they try to figure out solutions to all of the problems at hand, they are overwhelmed. Instead, they look for methods of problem solving. What kinds of styles have worked in the past? What kinds of people have they seen be successful? In this way, they can rely on their own experiences, the things they trust the most, to help them deal with the complexities of politics.

Not all of the people I spoke with used stylistic interpretations of politics to make sense of issues. Some people had relatively clear visions of how particular issues should be handled, and when an issue was raised, they judged political leaders and policies by how closely those leaders and policies matched their own solution.

Most of these people, though, had neither a purely stylistic nor a purely policy-oriented conception of politics. Rather, they had a mix of policy views and style views. The complexities of politics may tend to drive people away from issues and toward style, but most people try to understand politics by using a combination of these approaches.

Conclusions

The world of politics is an ambiguous place where people often see no easy solutions, feel overwhelmed by problems, or display contradictions in their views. Confusion is an ever-present element as individuals attempt to make sense of politics.

This confusion springs from a number of sources. Often there is too much information to comprehend, and this information glut is compounded by the low priority that many people give to politics. Some individuals feel incapable of developing any clear understanding of politics. Their feelings of personal inadequacy may prevent them from attempting to understand issues more fully.

In addition, confusion results from the conflicting goals that people have. They support democracy in the abstract, for example, but are distressed that some of the outcomes of that process conflict with other goals that they have. Thus, they may display ambivalence about democratic procedures. Similarly, their support of free speech may conflict with their support of fighting communism, and balancing the two may lead to confusion or ambivalence.

Finally, the sheer complexity and enormity of many political problems (such as keeping an economy moving or fighting drug abuse) create confusion. People often recognize social problems as problems that cannot be reduced to simple solutions.

People react to these feelings of confusion in a number of ways, and their reaction is partially a function of trust orientation. A common response of cynics is alienation from the system. In contrast, supporters often respond by trusting our leaders to do the right thing, at least in those policy areas where their feelings of confusion are greatest.

Another response is to try to recast complex policy issues into simple terms. Solving poverty problems becomes a matter of eliminating waste. Foreign policy issues become a matter of restoring American pride. The problem with this response, however, is that many people do recognize the complex problems underlying these issues, and they often turn to yet another approach: They rely on the politics of style.

If individuals do not know how to solve the drug problem or bring peace to the Middle East, they can look for a leader who has the kind of style they think will best lead to solutions. They know, often from their own experience, that strength or compassion or honesty, for example, is the best way to deal with problems. Rather than make sense of complex policy issues, they make sense of these problems in terms of the political style that is needed to achieve a desirable outcome.

8

Patterns of political thinking

They all laugh at angry young men.
They all laugh at Edison
and also at Einstein.
So why should I feel sorry
if they just couldn't understand
the idiomatic logic
that went on in my head.

—ANNIE ROSS and WARDELL GRAY

In order to make sense of politics and the world around them, people draw upon their own experiences. Their ideas about what is important are shaped by those experiences and the orientations that grow out of them. Their level of trust, the broadness of their vision, and their values all mold their view of the world. For many people the complexities and uncertainties of political issues, as well as the ways in which people relate their experiences to politics, cause them to rely on style and performance to make judgments. As we saw in Chapter 2, both party and ideological symbols can be seen in either policy or stylistic terms, but this distinction runs deeper. The basic approach that people take to politics can be distinguished in this way. For some people, politics consists of competing policy visions, but most people make sense of politics stylistically. For them, politics is about how we approach problems and how we relate to other people. If we take the proper approach, if we have the correct style, we are more likely to succeed.

Most of the people I talked to made sense of politics in stylistic, not policy, terms. Sixteen of them had primarily stylistic notions of the political world, and only eight had policy notions. (The other two had mixed notions.) Those with stylistic notions did have opinions on policies, and those with policy notions did have opinions about styles, but in judging political figures or explaining how particular problems were likely to be solved, some people relied most heavily on style, and others focused on policy.

Stylistic patterns of political thinking

Stylistic notions of politics are an attempt to make sense of a complicated and overwhelming world. Drawing on their own experiences, people look for leaders or policies that express the kinds of styles they think are likely to succeed. Stylistic notions of politics, then, are performance-oriented. Most people with such an orientation rely heavily on the success or failure of a policy to prove that the proper style has been followed. Paradoxically, style may be easy to judge because people can relate it to their own experiences, but it is also difficult to judge because it is hard to know if people actually act according to the proper style.

Thus, judgments about the success or failure of political figures are important in validating style judgments. If the economy seems to be going well, that is because the president is acting properly. He has the correct style. In contrast, policy-oriented individuals are much less performance-oriented. They focus not on the general success or failure of a political leader or policy but on the direction that policy has taken. Stylistic individuals are much more retrospective in a general sense. If things go well, positive style judgments are made; if not, negative judgments follow.

To some extent each individual has his or her own particular vision of style, but it was possible to find a number of common patterns among the people I interviewed. In fact, the sixteen stylistically oriented individuals fell into four different patterns of political thinking.

The most common of these patterns was what I call macho politics. Six people—Al Chambliss, Carl Figueroa, John Guidry, Bert Jackson, Amy Tidrow, and Gus White—had this pattern. For them, what was important was being tough. Probably the purest example was John. When I asked him what he liked about President Reagan, he replied, "His sternness." When I asked him what he had thought of Walter Mondale in the 1984 election, he said: "I don't think he was, just in some ways, I just don't think he was powerful enough. I think, more or less, he was a little laid-back, lax, where Reagan was a little bit more outgoing. And another thing that led me to my vote was Reagan's success in his four years before."

When I asked him about Governor Cuomo, he said:

> At first I didn't like Cuomo. But some of the things that he's starting to put into place, I think, are really helping the community as a whole or the state as a whole. I hated the seat-belt law to begin with. But now I just do it instamatically. It really doesn't matter. And I really do think it was a good law. . . . I think he's done a super job. I think what proves him strong is, issues no one else was willing to touch, he's touched. And that's the same thing as Reagan on the abortion issue. . . . And Cuomo on the seat-belt law and also the alcohol, raising the drinking age.

Strength was the key for John. Both a conservative Republican president and a liberal Democratic governor fit the bill. The proof was in their performance in office. Since things were going well, the importance of strength was confirmed. But for John, strength went beyond just a judgment of leaders. It also was reflected in John's approach to political issues. He believed that the United States should "get tough" in Nicaragua and that Star Wars should be "mandatory, not in a bargain," with the Russians. He argued that we should get tough with welfare recipients and not give things to them and that the way to fight the crime problem was "to charge up the chairs." He even saw abortion as a matter of being tough. He would allow abortion only in a case of rape because there the women had no choice:

> If a girl goes out and gets pregnant of her own accord, I would not grant her an abortion. . . . because making a decision is part of being a person. I think down the road it will make her a better person for it. . . . You have to live with

your decisions. If you get another job and you make a wrong decision, you can't abort it. That's a decision. I think the same thing should be done with sexuality courses. You have them, and you get pregnant—that's a decision you made.

The other five people with macho politics patterns had similar positions. Bert Jackson argued that it was a good thing for a leader to be ruthless. That had helped Richard Nixon succeed. In comparing Reagan and Carter, Bert noted: "Carter was just so lackadaisical. He couldn't do this. He couldn't do that. Reagan was going to straighten the country out. They needed someone who wasn't a wimp. They needed someone with some backbone. They wanted to restore pride in America." Amy Tidrow explained why she liked President Reagan: "He doesn't keep going back and forth, back and forth, like some other presidents have. Not that I really am too knowledgeable about political activity before this. I think he definitely sticks to what he thinks."

Carl Figueroa also compared Reagan's sternness to Carter's "wishy-washy" approach to politics. Carl's long discussion of the Vietnam War and how it had sparked his lifelong interest in international affairs was a lament over how the United States had not been strong enough in that situation. It was a war we should have won, and we would have won it if we had been tough enough.

Al Chambliss was in favor of being tough on welfare policy and crime, and he supported Ronald Reagan for being tough both in foreign policy and with Congress. But Al's macho politics orientation was tempered by a belief in the importance of sincerity. In discussing Ronald Reagan, Al noted his strength and then went on to say: "Here's a man who always has been involved, back in the fifties, et cetera. I think he's a sincere man. I think he really means well. Thank God we have him. I'm sure he's going to face some problems. He gets confused sometimes. But there's a man who is sincere."

Gus White's version of macho politics included a belief in fighting against the system. Gus liked Ronald Reagan because he was a "pistol-packing leader," but Gus's cynicism and almost complete alienation from the system led him to prefer people who used their strength to fight against the system. Despite his limited knowledge about most political issues, Gus mentioned that he liked

William Proxmire because Proxmire always tried to fight government waste. Most political leaders, in Gus's view, could not be trusted, but someone who was strong and willing to fight the system was good. Unfortunately, according to Gus, any president who was strong enough to really straighten things out "would not survive."

For these six people, the style of politics most likely to succeed was a politics of strength. The world was a tough place, and only the tough would get ahead. Political leaders and policies were judged to a large extent by how strong they were. Note how often references to strength were part of a judgment of a policy or the performance of an individual. By looking for strength (or for weakness when something was failing), these people made sense of the political world.

In almost complete contrast to macho politics was the second most common stylistic pattern, the politics of compassion. Five people had a compassionate pattern of thinking: Gail Blair, Adam Clay, Nancy Gullet, Ralph Randolph, and Carol Torrez. For them, political figures did not need to be tough, but they needed to care. They needed to be empathetic. Ralph, for example, preferred Jimmy Carter to Ronald Reagan: "[Carter] listened a little better, and he had a better ear listening to problems." Ralph also argued that we needed to do more to help the needy and that liberals were better than conservatives because liberals were "more for the people." Ralph's judgments about an individual's or a policy's compassion were based largely on an examination of how the individual or policy affected unemployment. If unemployment went up, leaders were not showing enough compassion. If it went down, their policies were judged a success. Thus, Ralph cited the rise in unemployment under Reagan as evidence that Reagan "does not care enough about the people," and the local unemployment situation was proof that local leaders were not doing enough. Ralph had other evidence of local leaders' inaction: "There is nothing going on here. It makes a big difference if you can get things to do for people. People got places to go, things to do. It makes a difference. On the weekends this town is dead. People go everywhere but here."

Likewise, Gail Blair expressed strong support for political figures who she thought were doing things to "help the people." She supported helping veterans and senior citizens, poor people and sick people. She argued that one of the major problems with the welfare system was that it did not treat people with respect, as was shown when her daughter was applying for aid under the WIC program: "They tell her to go to these places to clean these dirty holes. Who wants to go into a house and clean a house that's full of roaches and all that kind of crap? Come on." Gail was incensed that the French had refused to allow American bombers to use French airspace during a mission to bomb Libya, after "all we did for them" in World War II. (Paradoxically, she opposed the bombing itself because it was too risky.)

Adam Clay expressed disapproval of President Reagan because he was not doing enough to help the poor, although Adam did like "the way he talks to people" and that he was "understood by all the people." Adam supported Sherwood Boehlert, his local member of the House of Representatives, because he was "trying to help us."

The other two people with compassionate orientations tempered that compassion with a recognition of the importance of strength as well. Carol Torrez had the following to say about Jimmy Carter:

> I voted for him because I thought that he was great. Of course, I think he and Harry Truman sort of go together. And so many people thought that Harry Truman would not be big enough for the presidency. But there was a difference. Life had strengthened Truman in political ways, so he had strengths that were not easily seen by the average American. But those that were in the Congress knew. But Jimmy Carter had had things come rather easily to him. He hadn't been tried and tested, as it were. I'm afraid that he didn't have the strength of character to visit someone in jail, as Truman visited (was it Pendergast? he was in prison) because he had known him as a friend. He didn't necessarily approve. He wasn't in on the scheme. So I guess that was it. But I am sorry that Mr. Carter didn't succeed better.

Carol preferred the Democrats to Republicans because Democrats "live with the masses and understand them and therefore are more compassionate," but she also knew that leaders had to be strong to succeed.

Nancy Gullet liked both Ronald Reagan and Jimmy Carter because they both "wanted what was good for the country," and they both "cared." She thought that Reagan was a better president because Carter was "too easy" and perhaps Carter "should have been a priest."

Not surprisingly, there were important political differences between those with a compassionate pattern of political thinking and those with a macho pattern. Four of the six macho people (Bert, Carl, John, and Al) called themselves conservatives, but only one of the five with a compassionate orientation (Nancy) did so. On the other hand, two of those with a compassion orientation (Ralph and Carol) were liberals, and one (Adam) was a moderate. The others, Gail and Nancy, had no liberal-conservative identification. Of the other two with a macho orientation, Amy called herself a liberal, and Gus had no identification.

Although most people in these groups claimed independence when asked about party identification (something that generally tended to distinguish people with stylistic orientations from those with policy orientations), the two people with macho orientations who were not independent (Carl and Al) were Republicans, while the two with compassionate orientations who expressed a partisan identification (Ralph and Gail) were Democrats. All four of those who voted in 1984 and had a macho orientation voted for Ronald Reagan (Amy and Gus did not vote). Four of the five individuals with compassionate orientations did not vote in 1984. (Perhaps that helps to explain the size of the Reagan landslide!) Carol, the only one who did vote, voted for Ronald Reagan, though with great reluctance. She preferred Walter Mondale's "caring" but did not think he was "strong enough" for the job. And as we have just seen, she thought she had already made that mistake with Jimmy Carter.

It is also important to note the gender differences between these two styles of politics. Macho politics and compassion politics seemed to reflect common stereotypes of the differences in what men and women want in politics. The relationship was not perfect: One of those who preferred a macho style of politics was a woman, and two of those who looked for compassion were men. But there was a difference, and it reflected the findings of people such as Carol Gilligan who argue that women often speak with a "different voice."[1] According to Gilligan, men and women develop different perspectives on the world and often talk about the world in very different ways. Men often develop an ethic of rights that is based on self-reliance (strength), while women develop an ethic of care based on compassion and understanding. In her words, "Male and female voices typically speak of the importance of different truths, the former of the role of separation as it defines and empowers the self, the latter of the ongoing process of attachment that creates and sustains the human community."[2] It should not surprise us if such differences spill over into the way men and women make sense of politics.[3]

The other two stylistic patterns of thought were much less common. Three people—Martha Nettles, Dave Thomasson, and Carla Zeber—focused on honesty, and the other two—Tony Hunter and Laura Rivers—centered on diligence.

For Martha, Dave, and Carla, politics was about honesty and deceit. Martha explained why she did not vote for Walter Mondale: "He never convinced me. He never got a hundred percent of my trust." She thought Richard Nixon was a terrible president because of Watergate and that John Kennedy was the best president she could remember: "He just thought very clearly. Everything sounded so logical coming from him, which I admire in anyone. It's probably one of the things I admire about my boss today. He's very, very clear-thinking." Martha believed that our goal in foreign policy should be to convince other nations that we sincerely desired peace. If we could convince them of the honesty of our pronouncements, we could end much hostility. Her belief that Mikhail Gorbachev was honest led her to support negotiations with the Soviet Union. Martha's supportive orientation (trusting both the system and our leaders) predisposed her to support those in authority and believe the pronouncements of leaders. When nothing happened to contradict those instincts, she was likely to believe in the honesty and integrity of those in power and support whatever policies they offered. Only when things went badly, as with Watergate or the economy under Jimmy Carter, did she question the integrity of our leaders.

In contrast, Dave's search for honesty was coupled with a cynical trust orientation, so he had difficulty finding leaders he liked. He supported Walter Mondale in 1984:

> I think that he spoke right from the heart. He was a real honest-to-goodness man. And I just liked the way that he spoke out, and I thought that he was telling the truth. . . . But that tax deal is what crucified him. . . . He had to have taxation to a certain degree in order to meet the obligations of social security, welfare, old-age pensions, and all that stuff nobody can afford with a basket of more money. I mean it's got to be raised from the population. And I think that he was an honest man.

Dave also liked Senator Bill Bradley of New Jersey: "I don't know too much about him. I just know he might possibly could be an honest man. He doesn't seem to be a crook. He didn't throw ball games and stuff like that. I don't think a man becomes a crook overnight. I think the seed is planted quite early, and then it grows." On the other hand, he did not like Ted Kennedy because of Chappaquiddick, and he disliked Governor Cuomo because he "straddles the political fences." Dave noted that the most important thing about good leadership was honesty, but his cynicism made him doubt the honesty of our leaders and of the system.

Carla also placed honesty at the center of her political thinking, but she also emphasized hard work. She liked Jimmy Carter because he was honest and hardworking, and the two presidents she most admired were Franklin Roosevelt and Harry Truman because they "worked hard" and "stood by their beliefs." She would have preferred Gary Hart to Walter Mondale in 1984: "[Hart] seemed to be honest. Whatever he said seemed to be true." Richard Nixon was the worst president she could remember, because of Watergate.

Diligence was the central pattern of Tony Hunter and Laura Rivers. Both of them had a supportive trust orientation, so for them the key was to find individuals who would work hard. For Laura, it was important that leaders prove their diligence by working their way up through the system. Laura liked Governor Cuomo because "he's trying," and she liked Walter Mondale in 1984 because "he came up from the ranks." Jesse Jackson and Gary Hart, on the other hand, "came up too fast." At election time, Laura liked to look at the candidates' "biography or life story or a synopsis of it to see what he's accomplished or what he didn't accomplish."

Tony liked Ronald Reagan: "He is a go-getter. If he believes in something, he doesn't sit there and have somebody else do it. He goes out and tries to muster the votes and goes right to Congress and speaks to them. And he's not at all a man that appears to stand there and let the grass grow under his feet. He's got a lot of vigor for an older man." Tony contrasted that approach to Jimmy Carter's. He thought Carter was a bad president because he would "lay back and play a passive sort of person." Tony described what he looked for in a president: "Some guy that's not afraid to make a decision. Some guy or some woman, some person, who is willing to give one hundred and ten percent in the position that they're going for. Someone that's not there for the prestige about it but is there and wants to do a good job." For Tony, part of hard work was listening. He noted on a couple of occasions how important it was for political leaders to listen to their constituents. As we saw in Chapter 6, Tony's belief in the importance of listening came from his own experiences at work.

All sixteen of these people, then, tended to see politics in stylistic patterns. They found it easier to make sense of how politics works by focusing on leadership styles that they thought would be effective. Politicians or policies that reflected the appropriate style were likely to succeed, and those that did not were likely to fail. Furthermore, these patterns of thinking had a strong performance component, but by and large that performance was related back to style. It was hard to know if a leader or policy was really tough or compassionate or honest or hardworking until the results of that policy or that leader's actions were seen. Then the results became evidence that the proper style had or had not been followed.

Style, however, was not the only way that people related to politics. Some people thought about politics in terms of particular policies.

Policy patterns of political thinking

Eight individuals exhibited patterns of political thinking that focused on policy rather than style: Walter Beattie, Mark Dent, Sue Doyle, Mort Johnson, Clyde Lyle, Ted Munson, Simon Pinella, and Ed Stanley. They thought about politics in the way that classical democratic theory seems to imply all citizens should. They looked to see whether a political leader followed the policies that they preferred. They judged a policy by how closely it followed their perceptions of what was correct. All of them also noted the importance of style. Style might, for example, explain why a leader with a good policy failed. Thus, if Jimmy Carter had good ideas but could not succeed, it was because he was too weak. But when election time rolled around, a policy-oriented person who felt that way would still vote for Jimmy Carter.

Similarly, performance judgments by those with policy patterns of thinking were different from those with style patterns. Performance was much less crucial to policy-oriented people. It was more important that a leader or policy be heading in the correct direction than it was to succeed, if success meant moving in the wrong direction. Getting the economy moving was not enough, for example, if to do so we had to raise unemployment. Performance was judged in a directional manner.

Four of these people — Simon, Sue, Clyde, and Ed — had policy views that were basically conservative. Simon, for example, thought that people should work their way up in the world and should not be given money by the government. He supported getting tough on crime and scaling back on government. He supported Ronald Reagan over Walter Mondale because he preferred "to cut down on government spending," rather than have a tax increase, as a way to deal with the deficit. He thought Reagan was a good president despite his shortcomings: "He has probably bungled more speeches and said more wrong things and countries located in areas of the world where we never thought we were than any president before him, but . . . [he has been] moving the country in a positive direction."

Ed Stanley and Clyde Lyle supported less government and a strong stand against communism around the world, and they opposed gun control. They voted for Reagan over Mondale in 1984 because Reagan "supported better policies," in Ed's words, and "was more conservative," according to Clyde.

Sue Doyle, as we saw earlier, had a political approach that was based on doing what nature intended. She therefore opposed most government support of people, except in emergencies, because it interfered with people's reaching their natural level of ability. She also thought mothers should not work while the children are too young to go to school, because "nature intended for that woman to be with the child" (even though her own experience showed her that it could be frustrating and difficult for the woman). She was open to the idea that government might have a role to play in helping consumers fight the food industry, which she believed was feeding us chemicals rather than natural foods, but she was skeptical that government would actually do the job well. She thought government should not, and could not, try to impose equality.

In contrast, Walter Beattie, Mort Johnson, and Ted Munson were liberals. Ted wanted to cut military spending, increase social programs, end aid to the Contras, and increase the power of the poor and underprivileged in American society. Further, Ted said: "Ronald Reagan has the potential to be a very good leader if he would pay attention to what he was saying. His problem is that he talks without thinking very often. But he's got that magnetism personality. Jimmy Carter, I think, talked too much before he said anything and was afraid to make a decision or to do anything. He came off in the end as a bit of a wishy-washy kind of guy." Still, Ted supported Carter over Reagan in 1980.

Walter voted for Mondale in 1984, even though "I didn't think he was a very strong candidate," because "he was more for the average person than Reagan." Walter preferred Mondale's budget priorities and foreign-policy views. Mort voted for Carter over Reagan in 1980, even though Carter was "kind of slippery and wishy-washy," because he was the "lesser of two evils." Mort also thought we should spend less on the military and more on social services.

Mark Dent had an issue-oriented pattern of thinking that was neither liberal nor conservative. Rather, Mark's pattern was an eclectic mix based on his worldview. In some ways Mark was a libertarian (he had, you may recall, voted for the Libertarian candidate for president in 1976). He supported less government spending on both military and social programs and favored elimination of the income tax. He was strongly in favor of maintaining individual rights and had worried about the erosion of the rights of criminals in the Reagan years. But he also supported government as a watchdog in areas such as environmental quality and worker safety, so he was not willing to leave everything to the free market. His views are probably best summarized as revolving around protecting individuals and their liberty. Government involvement was possible, but only to help individuals fight for their rights.

These eight people were divided in their policy positions. The four conservatives voted for Reagan in 1984, and the three liberals plus Mark voted for Mondale. The four conservatives identified themselves as Republicans, and three of them identified themselves as conservatives (Sue called herself a moderate), while the three liberals identified themselves as Democrats, and two of them identified themselves as liberals (Walter called himself a moderate). Mark identified himself as an independent and a moderate.

People with policy patterns of political thinking are the kinds of people we search for in most of the surveys that we do. They fit the patterns we look for, and their views tend to be consistent with the categories of analysis (such as party and ideology) that we tend to use. But if the people I talked with are at all representative, people with policy patterns of thinking are vastly outnumbered by those with stylistic patterns of thought.

Before exploring some of the differences that emerged between individuals with these two patterns, let me briefly say something about the other two people I talked with: Howard Gossage and George Heath. Both of these men had mixed patterns of thought. As I noted earlier, everyone has a mixed pattern to some extent, but in most cases it is possible (and relatively easy) to see whether style or policy is more central. For Howard and George, that was not the case. Both of them talked a lot about style; in particular, both tended toward macho politics as they discussed the importance of being tough and having strong leaders. On the other hand, when it came to judging the performance of political leaders or policies, there was an important policy dimension in their thinking. Howard was clear that particular budget priorities needed to be followed; otherwise it did not matter how strong a leader was. George judged performance by a wide range of specific policy criteria. But this policy dimension was also not predominant. Neither man judged candidates by the policies they promised, because neither man believed these promises. In judging candidates, Howard and George relied on a combination of style and policy, with policy being retrospective but in a specific direction, not the more general nature found in most stylistic individuals.

Differences between stylistic and policy patterns

Both educational and interest-level differences were present between people with stylistic patterns and those with policy patterns. As table 8.1 indicates, better-educated people were more likely to have policy patterns of thinking. None of the individuals with less than a high school education, and only one person with no more than a high school degree (Sue), had a policy pattern. Education did not ensure a policy pattern: Half of the college graduates and one of the people with an advanced degree (Bert) had a stylistic orientation. But education did increase the likelihood of a policy pattern of thinking. We have seen that it is often the ambiguities and complexities of politics that force people to rely on stylistic criteria, so such a result is not surprising.

Greater interest in politics also seems to be associated with a policy-oriented pattern (see table 8.2). Three of the five people with high interest have a policy orientation, while most of those with less interest have a stylistic orientation. The effect of interest is

Table 8.1. Relationship between interviewees' pattern of thought and education

| Education | Pattern of thought | | |
	Style	Policy	Total
Grade school	3	0	3
Some high school	2	0	2
High school	4	1	5
Some college	3	2	5
College	3	3	6
Advanced degree	1	2	3
Total	16	8	24

Note: Figures are the numbers of people fitting each category. Two people (one with a high school education and one with some college) had a mixed pattern of thought.

Table 8.2. Relationship between interviewees' pattern of thought and interest in politics

Interest in politics	Pattern of thought		
	Style	Policy	Total
Low	5	2	7
Moderate	9	3	12
High	2	3	5
Total	16	8	24

Note: Figures are the numbers of people fitting each category. Two people (one with moderate interest and one with high interest) had a mixed pattern of thought.

not as clear as that of education, but interest does seem to be a factor. (Given the size of this sample, however, none of these relationships is conclusive.)

There are also some intriguing relationships between patterns of thought and some of the other underlying orientations we have looked at. With regard to trust orientation, five of the eight people with a policy orientation were skeptics. (The other three are split among the other three categories). A trust of individuals but not of the system seems to be the most likely orientation of those who see politics in terms of policy. It is striking that a majority of the skeptics (five of nine) have policy patterns, while the vast bulk of cynics (five of seven, with one other being mixed) and supporters (six of seven) — those with complete trust or complete distrust — had stylistic patterns. (The three democrats, who trust the system but not our leaders, were evenly divided: Ralph had a style pattern, Ed had a policy pattern, and George had a mixed pattern.) It seems that skepticism, or possibly even ambivalence over whether one can trust the system and our leaders, allows for a policy perspective. Perhaps complete trust or complete distrust in both the system and our leaders leads to an attitude of not having to worry about policies. Either things will always work out in the end or they will never work out in the end, so there is not much point in looking at the policy details. The best that can be done is to try to find those types of leaders who are most likely to succeed or, as the cynics would put it, least likely to be corrupt. The disjunction between the system and leaders may make the details of policy more important. I would not want to push this speculation too far, though. The numbers are small, and the relationship is far from perfect, but the differences are striking.

In terms of scope orientation, the one figure that stands out is that four of the five people with an international orientation had a stylistic pattern of thought. Given the difficulties of learning about the details of foreign policy and relating those details to one's own experience (the most common way for people to make sense of politics), it is not surprising that people who focus on international politics will rely most heavily on stylistic patterns of response to the events that concern them. The exception to this was Simon, who had a policy orientation despite his international perspective. Each of the other scope orientations is amenable to either a stylistic or a policy pattern. Of the eight people with a local orientation, four had a stylistic pattern, three had a policy pattern, and one was mixed. The eight people with national orientations were evenly divided between stylistic and policy patterns of thinking.

Finally, in terms of value orientation, there does not seem to be any clear pattern present. People with a policy orientation were split relatively evenly across the four value orientations, and the same was true of those with a stylistic orientation. The one possible exception was that three of the four individualists had a policy pattern.

It is difficult in such a small sample to sort out all of these relationships, but it is clear that people's pattern of political thinking affects the kinds of things they pay attention to, the qualities they look for in leaders, and the kinds of evidence they seek. Knowing whether someone focuses on policy or style, then, can tell us a lot about the way he or she approaches politics. Before concluding this look at how people make sense of politics, let us briefly explore the 1984 American National Election Study, done by the Center for Political Studies, for some further evidence that this distinction between policy and stylistic patterns is an important and useful one.

Stylistic and policy patterns
in the American public

The data available in large surveys of the American public are not easliy adapted for making the kinds of distinctions I have been making between people with stylistic and policy patterns of political thinking. Closed-ended, forced-choice questions do not lend themselves to an analysis of how people make sense of politics. We may be able to know what their opinion is on a particular issue or whether they like a particular candidate, but why that might be so is much harder to decipher. Nonetheless, if we want to understand the dynamics of public opinion, we need to understand the patterns of thought that people have and how these patterns affect the ways people approach political issues and candidates.[4]

The usefulness of distinguishing among people on the basis of how they think about politics can be seen in data from the 1984 American National Election Survey. Even using relatively crude measures of stylistic and policy patterns of thinking, it is possible to detect major differences in how people evaluate political leaders.

In order to explore the importance of stylistic and policy patterns of thinking in the broad public, I examined people's responses to the question of what they liked and disliked about the two major political parties. My twenty-six interviews indicated that there was a strong correlation between people's perceptions of the parties and their overall pattern of political thinking. Of the twenty-six people I talked with, none had orientations toward the parties that did not match, at least in part, their pattern of political thinking, so I added up the number of stylistic references and the number of policy references in the national-survey responses to the question of likes and dislikes about the parties.[5]

Admittedly, this is a crude measure. The Interuniversity Consortium for Political and Social Research did not code responses with this distinction in mind, and many of the codes they assigned were difficult to label as stylistic or policy-oriented. (For a complete list of the coding, see Appendix E). For example, I chose to code all references to specific individuals or groups within a party as stylistic responses because that tended to be the pattern among the people I talked with. However, that system obviously misclassified some policy responses, particularly among group references. On the other hand, I coded all responses using ideological labels as policy responses, again because that was most often the case among the people I talked with. Here, too, some stylistic responses must have been misclassified. I then classified each individual as having a style pattern or a policy pattern according to whether that person had more style or policy references. Anyone with an equal number of responses in the two categories was classified as mixed, and I classified anyone who did not like or dislike anything about either party as stylistic, because nine of the ten people in my study with no party orientation had a stylistic pattern of thinking, while the tenth was mixed.[6]

Using this scheme, 68 percent of the sample was classified as stylistic, 24 percent as policy-oriented, and 8 percent as mixed. This distribution was relatively similar to the one I found in my smaller, in-depth sample. As table 8.3 indicates, the educational distribution also reflected the findings of my study, with better-educated people being more likely to exhibit policy patterns of thinking. The relationship was not perfect; there was a slight decline in the percentage of policy individuals from college graduates to those who went on for an advanced degree (35 percent to 33 percent).

Table 8.3. Relationship of subjects' pattern of thought and education in a national sample

	Subjects (%)	
Education	Style-oriented	Policy-oriented
Grade school	78	17
Some high school	75	18
High school	72	20
Some college	63	28
College	56	35
Advanced degree	62	33

Note: Data are from the 1984 American National Election Study, by the Center for Political Studies, and were made available through the Interuniversity Consortium for Political and Social Research. Percentages are by row. People with mixed patterns were not included.

I then attempted to measure how people thought about the two presidential candidates, Ronald Reagan and Walter Mondale. Regression analyses were performed, using people's feelings about Reagan and Mondale as the dependent variables. In order to test people's feelings about political leaders, respondents were asked to rate their attitudes along a "feeling thermometer," which ran from zero for those who did not like the candidate at all, to 50 for those with no feelings one way or the other, to 100 for those with strong positive feelings about the candidate in question.[7] For each candidate, two separate regressions were run, one for people with style patterns and one for those with policy patterns. If the argument made in this book is correct, then we would expect differences to emerge between the stylistic and policy-oriented individuals in terms of which factors were important in helping them reach their judgments about the candidates.

Four independent variables were used (see Appendix E for a full accounting of the construction of these variables). The object was not to find an equation that explained the greatest amount of variance in how people thought about these candidates. Rather, the object was to compare the relative influence of different factors for people with style and policy patterns. Thus, only the most relevant variables were used.

First was a measure of personality. I considered people's responses to a series of questions about how well certain qualities — such as good leadership, morals, commands respect, and hard-working — described the candidates in question. Fifteen qualities were listed for each candidate, and a scale was created that ran from 30 if the candidate was well described by all of the qualities to −30 if these qualities did not describe the candidate at all.[8] Because the dependent variable was a measure of feelings about a candidate, we would expect that a candidate's personality would be important for people with both stylistic and policy orientations, though it might be slightly more important for those with a stylistic orientation.

Second was a measure of closeness on the issues. This score was the average distance the respondent saw between himself or herself and the candidate on a series of seven issues. For each of these issues, respondents located their own position and then identified where they thought Mondale and Reagan belonged on the scale. Scores for each issue could run from zero (if the respondents thought their position matched a candidate's) to 6 (if the respondents placed themselves at the opposite end of the issue from the candidate). The scale did not take direction of difference into account; for example, being one place more liberal than Mondale was the same as being one place more conservative. A respondent's total score on the scale was the average distance between the respondent and the candidate for all of the questions for which the respondent was able to place both himself or herself and the candidate. Only people who could not place either themselves or the candidate on all seven questions were treated as missing data.[9] Because the variable measured distance between the candidate and the respondent, the regression coefficient should be negative. We would also expect issue distance to be more important for people with policy patterns than for those with style patterns.

The third independent variable was party identification. The standard 7-point party identification scale running from strong Democrat (0) to independent (3) to strong Republican (6) was used. Thus, because higher scores indicate more Republican respondents, we should get positive regression coefficients for Reagan and negative regression coefficients for Mondale. Given the findings in my interviews, we would expect partisanship to be more important for respondents with policy patterns of thinking. There was a strong consistency between partisanship and feelings about candidates for policy individuals, whereas those with style patterns were much less consistent. This is probably because it is much easier to find examples of the "correct" styles in each party than it is to find examples of the "correct" policy mix in each party. People with stylistic patterns, then, would tend to rely less on partisanship when evaluating political candidates.

The fourth independent variable was a retrospective evaluation of the current (Reagan) administration. This measure was a combination of a respondent's evaluations of how good a job Reagan was doing and how well the government was handling whatever the respondent saw as the most important problem in the nation.[10] The scale runs from 2 for those who strongly approved of the job Reagan was doing and thought the government was doing a good job of solving whatever they thought was the nation's most important problem to 10 for those who strongly disapproved of the job Reagan was doing and thought the government was doing a poor job of solving the nation's major problem. (Thus we should get negative coefficients for Reagan and positive coefficients for Mondale.) We would expect that this factor would be much more important for people with a style pattern than for policy-oriented people, because style-oriented people rely heavily on retrospective evaluations to validate that the "proper" style is being used, whereas policy-oriented people are much less reliant on such evaluations.

It was difficult to know what to do with the retrospective evaluation questions in the Mondale equations, because there were no questions asking for an evaluation of Mondale's career. In fact, when a challenger runs against an incumbent, there is typically such an imbalance in the information that people have. They know more about the incumbent. However, one might expect that people who are dissatisfied with the way things are going would be more likely to find any challenger more attractive. How people judge the current administration will affect the way they see any challenges to it. Additionally, comparing results across different regression equations is much more complicated if the equations are not identical. Thus, the scale for the retrospective evaluation of Reagan was retained in the Mondale equation, with the exception that its effects would be limited.

Table 8.4 shows the results of these regression analyses, and the results were for the most part what we would expect.[11] Personality was the most important factor in all four equations and

Table 8.4. Effects of factors on subjects' attitudes toward Reagan and Mondale in a national sample

Independent variable	Attitude toward Reagan		Attitude toward Mondale	
	Style-oriented subjects	Policy-oriented subjects	Style-oriented subjects	Policy-oriented subjects
Personality	.82*	.79*	.66*	.65*
	(.05)	(.08)	(.09)	(.07)
	[.46]	[.42]	[.22]	[.32]
Issue closeness	−2.9*	−4.7*	−2.0*	−4.1*
	(.49)	(.80)	(1.1)	(.76)
	[−.14]	[−.22]	[−.05]	[−.21]
Party identification	1.2*	2.2*	−1.7*	−3.8*
	(.24)	(.40)	(.54)	(.49)
	[.10]	[.17]	[−.10]	[−.35]
Retrospective evaluation of Reagan administration	−2.6*	−1.9*	2.4*	.38
	(.28)	(.41)	(.45)	(.40)
	[−.25]	[−.17]	[.17]	[.04]
R^2	.66	.76	.15	.52

Note: Data are from the 1984 American National Election Study. Regression coefficients are presented. Figures in parentheses are standard errors; figures in brackets are standardized coefficients.
*$p < .01$.

seemed to have essentially the same effect for both style- and policy-oriented people.[12] But the other factors varied just as we would expect. Issues were much more important for policy-oriented people than for style-oriented people. For Mondale the coefficient for issue distance was twice as high for people with policy patterns as for those with style patterns; in fact, the coefficient for those with style patterns was not even statistically significant. For Reagan the difference was also great.

Retrospective evaluations were more important for those with a stylistic pattern of thinking than for those with a policy pattern. The retrospective evaluations in the Mondale equation were not even statistically significant for policy-oriented individuals, and in the Reagan equation, where the question was clearly more relevant, the coefficient was greater for those with style patterns. In addition, although retrospective evaluations were clearly the second most important factor in how those with a stylistic pattern evaluated Reagan, they were weakest, or were tied for being the weakest, factor for those with a policy pattern.

Partisanship was much more important among those with a policy pattern. For Mondale the party identification coefficient was more than twice as great for people with a policy pattern as for those with a style pattern, and for Reagan the coefficient was almost twice as great.

Obviously, the factors that people take into account when they judge political figures are influenced by their pattern of political thinking. By using the information gathered from in-depth discussions with people, we are better able to understand the patterns that emerge in survey data. And by using these two techniques in tandem, we are better able to get a handle on how people make sense of politics and the applicability of such patterns to the population as a whole. Even using the crude measures created here, patterns emerged as we expected. If it were easier to use these surveys to discover peoples' patterns of thought, I would expect that the differences would be even greater.

Conclusions

People do try to make sense of politics, even though it may not be a high priority and they may find it difficult to understand. We may not be a nation of involved, highly informed individuals with opinions on all the issues of the day, but neither are we a nation of people who simply support the person who looks the best on television. Many people rely on stylistic clues to help them figure out what is going on, but those clues are not the result of indifference or whim. Stylistic clues are, for many people, a way to relate their own experiences and knowledge to politics.[13] They are used to sorting out what works and what does not, and retrospective evaluations of success or failure, as such clues, are a crucial element of stylistic thinking. A politician's media image may help initially. People do look for strength or compassion, for example. Their experiences tell them that tough people or compassionate people are likely to succeed. (The different styles people look for also seem to reflect socialization and developmental patterns, with men and women tending to look for different patterns.) But eventually people look to a politician's results to see if the "proper" style is being used.

This is not to say that people rely exclusively on style or policies. Rather, as they sort through the world, many focus on style. They may still have opinions on issues of concern to them, but style seems to them to be more relevant than any particular policy position. In a similar way, those who focus on policy (a minority, but their numbers are substantial) do not ignore style. They recognize that the ways in which leaders act can be important to success or failure, but they care more about positions and the direction of politics than about the styles. Their evaluations are markedly different from those made by style-oriented people.

Still, I would not want the distinction to seem too stark. Most people try to find a balance of style and policy. Most style-oriented people, even those who look for the style we called macho politics, would object to a strong leader who took away too many of their freedoms. And there is a limit to how much ineffectiveness policy-oriented people will accept in a leader, even one who is moving in the right direction. Each individual has a unique mix of these factors.

Some other fundamental factors help shape the way that people make sense of politics. People's trust orientation helps them decide who or what they can trust. Some people have no faith in our leaders to do the right thing; they think all people are corrupt. Others see all of our leaders as basically good. These attitudes interact with attitudes toward the system. For some, the system itself is corrupting. For others, the system keeps things honest. People's attitudes on a whole host of issues are shaped by their underlying feelings of trust and distrust.

Similarly, the scope with which people view politics affects their attitudes. For some, politics is a local concern. Others know much about national politics but little about local affairs. Still others focus on international politics. Scope is more than just knowledge. Some individuals follow politics at all levels but focus on one level. The focus of people's politics, what political arena they see as relevant, is also important in helping shape people's political attitudes.

Finally, people's values — the mix of attitudes that they have toward freedom, equality, and opportunity — shape their approach to politics. Although most Americans support equality of opportunity as the ultimate goal of the system, a fair number of people are more egalitarian, more individualistic, or more focused on freedom. People with different values often have different political agendas. Additionally, how well people think the system has done in reaching these goals has an impact on their political attitudes.

Because politics is often complicated and confusing, people prefer to rely on their own experiences as a guide, but that does not mean people are guided only by self-interest. Rather they are guided, as best they can be, by their sense of what is fair. Because most people have only limited experiences to draw on, those values are often self-interested. But when self-interest and fairness conflict, people are willing to make sacrifices for the larger good.

Making sense of politics was not easy for most of the people I spoke with. They struggled with the complexities and ambiguities of the world, and they were confused by experts on all sides of questions. As a result, they often fell back on the things they trusted most — their own experiences. If we are to understand the dynamics of public opinion, we cannot be content with analysts' categories. We cannot simply look to people's partisanship or ideology or evaluations of the president or opinions on issues. Instead we need to get a better sense of how people relate what happens in politics to what happens in their own lives. I hope that this study is a beginning in that direction.

By understanding how people make sense of politics, we can make better sense of our democracy and its strengths and weaknesses. The public may seem to be moved by things that are ephemeral and unimportant. "Style is no substitute for substance" is a lament we often hear about contemporary American democracy and the problems that it faces. But if the public is moved by style, it is because it sees style as instrumental in achieving substance. In the end, people do demand performance. People are not simply satisfied with the "right" style. The proof of the pudding, as they say, is in the eating. In the day-to-day world of most people — a complicated world where they have to struggle with their own immediate problems before they can think about political problems and where the time and energy needed to understand issues is rarely available — such a method of making sense of politics really is not so surprising, nor, from a democratic perspective, is it so bad.

Demographic and political profile of interview subjects

Education			Sex	
Grade school	3 (12%)		Male	18 (69%)
Some high school	3 (12%)		Female	8 (31%)
High school	5 (19%)			
Some college	6 (23%)		**Religion**	
College	6 (23%)		Protestant	8 (31%)
Advanced degree	3 (12%)		Catholic	17 (66%)*
			Jewish	1 (4%)
Party Identification				
Democrat	8 (31%)		**Age**	
Republican	6 (23%)		Under 25	4 (15%)
Independent	12 (46%)		26–35	6 (23%)
			36–45	3 (12%)
Political Interest			46–55	4 (15%)
High	6 (23%)		56–65	4 (15%)
Moderate	13 (50%)		Over 65	5 (19%)
Low	7 (27%)			

Ideological Identification
Liberal   6 (24% of total;
                   29% of those with an identification)
Moderate   6 (24%; 29%)
Conservative   9 (36%; 43%)
None   4 (15%)

Presidential Vote in 1984**
Reagan   14 (70% of those voting)
Mondale   6 (30%)

---

*One was a Maronite Catholic, not a Roman Catholic.
**Turnout in 1984 was 20 out of 26 or 76%.

Characteristics of interview subjects

Walter Beattie

Age: 56
Religion: Jewish
Occupation: White-collar worker
1984 vote: Mondale
Ideological identification: Moderate
Partisan orientation: Policy
Scope orientation: National
Political orientation: Policy (liberal)

Education: Some college
Marital status: Married (2 grown children)
Interest in politics: Low
Party identification: Democrat
Ideological orientation: Policy (social)
Trust orientation: Skeptic
Value orientation: Equality of opportunity (need more)

Gail Blair

Age: 50
Religion: Catholic
Occupation: Unemployed (on total disability)
1984 vote: Did not vote
Ideological identification: None
Partisan orientation: Style
Scope orientation: Local
Political orientation: Style (compassion)

Education: Some high school
Marital status: Divorced (3 grown children)
Interest in politics: Moderate
Party identification: Democrat
Ideological orientation: None
Trust orientation: Cynic
Value orientation: Egalitarianism

Al Chambliss

Age: 40
Religion: Catholic
Occupation: Small business owner
1984 vote: Reagan
Ideological identification: Conservative
Partisan orientation: Style and policy
Scope orientation: Local
Political orientation: Style (macho)

Education: College
Marital status: Married (2 children)
Interest in politics: High
Party identification: Republican
Ideological orientation: Policy (economic)
Trust orientation: Skeptic
Value orientation: Equality of opportunity (gone too far)

Adam Clay

Age: 20
Religion: Catholic
Occupation: College student
1984 vote: Did not vote
Ideological identification: Moderate
Partisan orientation: None
Scope orientation: Mixed (national and local)
Political orientation: Style (compassion)

Education: Some college (still enrolled)
Marital status: Single
Interest in politics: Low
Party identification: Independent
Ideological orientation: Style
Trust orientation: Supporter
Value orientation: Egalitarianism

Mark Dent

Age: 39
Religion: Catholic
Occupation: Manual laborer
1984 vote: Mondale
Ideological identification: Moderate
Partisan orientation: Style and policy
Scope orientation: National
Political orientation: Policy (libertarian)

Education: Some college
Marital status: Married (2 children)
Interest in politics: Moderate
Party identification: Independent
Ideological orientation: Policy (general)
Trust orientation: Cynic
Value orientation: Libertarianism

Sue Doyle

Age: 34
Religion: Catholic
Occupation: Homemaker and part-time self-employment
1984 vote: Reagan
Ideological identification: Moderate
Partisan orientation: Policy
Scope orientation: Local
Political orientation: Policy (conservative)

Education: High school
Marital status: Married (1 child)
Interest in politics: Low
Party identification: Republican
Ideological orientation: Style
Trust orientation: Skeptic
Value orientation: Individualism

Carl Figueroa

Age: 35
Religion: Protestant
Occupation: Manual laborer
1984 vote: Reagan
Ideological identification: Conservative
Partisan orientation: Style and policy
Scope orientation: International
Political orientation: Style (macho)

Education: High school
Marital status: Single
Interest in politics: High
Party identification: Republican
Ideological orientation: Style and policy
Trust orientation: Cynic
Value orientation: Libertarianism

Howard Gossage

Age: 68
Religion: Protestant
Occupation: Retired (manual laborer)
1984 vote: Reagan
Ideological identification: Conservative
Partisan orientation: None
Scope orientation: Local
Political orientation: Mix

Education: Some high school
Marital status: Married (4 grown children)
Interest in politics: Moderate
Party identification: Independent
Ideological orientation: Policy (economic)
Trust orientation: Cynic
Value orientation: Equality of opportunity (gone too far)

John Guidry

Age: 27
Religion: Catholic
Occupation: Salesperson
1984 vote: Reagan
Ideological identification: Conservative
Partisan orientation: None
Scope orientation: International
Political orientation: Style (macho)

Education: College
Marital status: Married (no children)
Interest in politics: Moderate
Party identification: Independent
Ideological orientation: Style
Trust orientation: Supporter
Value orientation: Equality of opportunity (gone too far)

Nancy Gullet

Age: 79
Religion: Protestant
Occupation: Retired (homemaker)
1984 vote: Did not vote
Ideological identification: Conservative
Partisan orientation: None
Scope orientation: National
Political orientation: Style (compassion)

Education: Grade school
Marital status: Widow (3 grown children)
Interest in politics: Moderate
Party identification: Independent
Ideological orientation: Style
Trust orientation: Supporter
Value orientation: Equality of opportunity (okay)

George Heath

Age: 59
Religion: Catholic
Occupation: Retired (government employee)
1984 vote: Reagan
Ideological identification: Moderate
Partisan orientation: Style and policy
Scope orientation: Mixed (national and local)
Political orientation: Mix

Education: Some college
Marital status: Separated (3 grown children)
Interest in politics: High
Party identification: Democrat
Ideological orientation: Style
Trust orientation: "democrat"
Value orientation: Equality of opportunity (okay)

Tony Hunter

Age: 38
Religion: Catholic
Occupation: manual laborer
1984 vote: Reagan
Ideological identification: Moderate
Partisan orientation: Style
Scope orientation: National
Political orientation: Style (diligence)

Education: Some college
Marital status: Married (3 children)
Interest in politics: Moderate
Party identification: Independent
Ideological orientation: Style
Trust orientation: Supporter
Value orientation: Equality of opportunity (okay)

Bert Jackson

Age: 40
Religion: Catholic
Occupation: Health care professional
1984 vote: Reagan
Ideological identification: Conservative
Partisan orientation: None
Scope orientation: Mixed (none)
Political orientation: Style (macho)

Education: Advanced degree
Marital status: Married (1 child)
Interest in politics: Moderate
Party identification: Independent
Ideological orientation: Style and
 policy
Trust orientation: Cynic
Value orientation: Libertarianism

Mort Johnson

Age: 61
Religion: Protestant
Occupation: Government employee
1984 vote: Mondale
Ideological identification: Liberal
Partisan orientation: Policy
Scope orientation: National
Political orientation: Policy (liberal)

Education: Advanced degree
Marital status: Married (4 grown
 children)
Interest in politics: High
Party identification: Democrat
Ideological orientation: Policy (social)
Trust orientation: Skeptic
Value orientation: Egalitarianism

Clyde Lyle

Age: 24
Religion: Catholic
Occupation: Unemployed
1984 vote: Reagan
Ideological identification: Conservative
Partisan orientation: Policy
Scope orientation: National
Political orientation: Policy (conservative)

Education: College
Marital status: Married (no children)
Interest in politics: Moderate
Party identification: Republican
Ideological orientation: Policy (social)
Trust orientation: Skeptic
Value orientation: Individualism

Ted Munson

Age: 34
Religion: Protestant
Occupation: White-collar worker
1984 vote: Mondale
Ideological identification: Liberal
Partisan orientation: Style and policy
Scope orientation: Local
Political orientation: Policy (liberal)

Education: Advanced degree
Marital status: Married (3 children)
Interest in politics: Moderate
Party identification: Democrat
Ideological orientation: Policy (general)
Trust orientation: Skeptic
Value orientation: Egalitarianism

Martha Nettles

Age: 52
Religion: Catholic
Occupation: Secretary
1984 vote: Reagan
Ideological identification: Liberal
Partisan orientation: Style
Scope orientation: International
Political orientation: Style (honesty)

Education: High school
Marital status: Separated (4 children — 2 grown)
Interest in politics: Some
Party identification: Independent
Ideological orientation: Style
Trust orientation: Supporter
Value orientation: Individualism

Simon Pinella

Age: 25
Religion: Catholic
Occupation: White-collar worker
1984 vote: Reagan
Ideological identification: Conservative
Partisan orientation: Policy
Scope orientation: International
Political orientation: Policy (conservative)

Education: College
Marital status: Single
Interest in politics: High
Party identification: Republican
Ideological orientation: Policy (general)
Trust orientation: Supporter
Value orientation: Individualism

Ralph Randolph

Age: 28
Religion: Catholic
Occupation: Unemployed (manual laborer)
1984 vote: Did not vote
Ideological identification: Liberal
Partisan orientation: None
Scope orientation: National
Political orientation: Style (compassion)

Education: High school
Marital status: Married (1 child)
Interest in politics: Low
Party identification: Democrat
Ideological orientation: Style
Trust orientation: "democrat"
Value orientation: Equality of opportunity (need more)

Laura Rivers

Age: 64
Religion: Maronite Catholic
Occupation: Retired (homemaker, clerical worker)
1984 vote: Mondale
Ideological identification: None
Partisan orientation: None
Scope orientation: Mixed (national and local)
Political orientation: Style (diligence)

Education: High school
Marital status: Widow (3 grown children)
Interest in politics: Low
Party identification: Democrat
Ideological orientation: None
Trust orientation: Supporter
Value orientation: Equality of opportunity (okay)

Ed Stanley

Age: 33
Religion: Protestant
Occupation: White-collar worker
1984 vote: Reagan
Ideological identification: Conservative
Partisan orientation: Style and policy
Scope orientation: Local
Political orientation: Policy (conservative)

Education: College
Marital status: Married (1 child)
Interest in politics: High
Party identification: Republican
Ideological orientation: Style and policy
Trust orientation: "democrat"
Value orientation: Equality of opportunity (gone too far)

Dave Thomasson

Age: 77
Religion: Catholic
Occupation: Part-time service worker
1984 vote: Mondale
Ideological identification: None
Partisan orientation: None
Scope orientation: International
Political orientation: Style (honesty)

Education: Grade school
Marital status: Married (3 grown children)
Interest in politics: Low
Party identification: Democrat
Ideological orientation: None
Trust orientation: Cynic
Value orientation: Libertarianism

Amy Tidrow

Age: 20
Religion: Protestant
Occupation: College student and part-time skilled laborer
1984 vote: Did not vote
Ideological identification: Liberal
Partisan orientation: Style
Scope orientation: Mixed (national and local)
Political orientation: Style (macho)

Education: Some college (still enrolled)
Marital status: Single
Interest in politics: Moderate
Party identification: Independent
Ideological orientation: Style
Trust orientation: Skeptic
Value orientation: Individualism

Carol Torrez

Age: 80
Religion: Catholic
Occupation: Retired schoolteacher
1984 vote: Reagan
Ideological identification: Liberal
Partisan orientation: Style
Scope orientation: National
Political orientation: Style (compassion)

Education: College
Marital status: Single
Interest in politics: Some
Party identification: Independent
Ideological orientation: Style
Trust orientation: Skeptic
Value orientation: Equality of opportunity (need more)

Gus White

Age: 53
Religion: Catholic
Occupation: Unemployed (manual laborer)
1984 vote: Did not vote
Ideological identification: None
Partisan orientation: None
Scope orientation: Local
Political orientation: Style (macho)

Education: Some high school
Marital status: Married (5 grown children)
Interest in politics: Low
Party identification: Independent
Ideological orientation: None
Trust orientation: Cynic
Value orientation: Equality of opportunity (okay)

Carla Zeber

Age: 67
Religion: Protestant
Occupation: Retired (homemaker, government employee)
1984 vote: Reagan
Ideological identification: None
Partisan orientation: None
Scope orientation: Local
Political orientation: Style (honesty)

Education: Grade school
Marital status: Married (6 grown children)
Interest in politics: Some
Party identification: Independent
Ideological orientation: None
Trust orientation: Skeptic
Value orientation: Libertarianism

Questions asked in interviews

The following questions about politics (as well as a number of demographic questions) were asked in all of the interviews. The order varied, depending on the course of the interview. Also, if someone volunteered the information sought with these questions before they were asked, I did not repeat the question but went on to probe the meaning of the response. For example, if in discussing his interest in politics, a man said, "I am interested because I am a Republican and I like to follow the fortunes of the Republican party," I did not ask the first part of the party identification question. Rather, when he had finished talking about his interest in politics, I would say something like: "You said you are a Republican. Would you call yourself a strong Republican or a not very strong Republican?" After he answered that question, I would go on to explore what he thought it meant to support the Republican party. Similarly, if someone alluded to one of these issues without prompting, my question would follow from the allusion but would not be asked in the exact wording given below.

Interest in politics
- Would you say you are very much interested in government and politics, somewhat interested, or not very interested?
- Where do you get most of your information about politics?

Party identification
- Generally speaking, do you think of yourself as a Republican, a Democrat, an Independent, or what?
- (Asked of partisans:) Would you call yourself a strong Republican (Democrat) or a not very strong Republican (Democrat)?

- (Asked of Independents:) Do you think of yourself as closer to the Republican or Democratic party?
- Do you think there are any differences between the Democrats and the Republicans? (If yes:) What are they?

Ideological identification

- We hear a lot of talk these days about liberals and conservatives. Would you say that you are a liberal, a moderate, a conservative, or don't you know?
- What do you think (do you think others think) it means to be a liberal (conservative) in politics today?
- Do you think either party is more conservative than the other? (If yes:) Which party is more conservative? What do you mean when you say that?

Trust in government

- How much of the time do you think you can trust the government to do what is right? Why?
- Do you think that the government wastes tax money? (If yes:) Where do you think this waste occurs? Why do you think this waste occurs?

Tax reform

- There is talk these days about reforming the tax system. Have you heard anything about this issue? (If yes:) What do you think about these proposals?

Evaluations of political leaders

- Do you think Ronald Reagan has been a good president? Why (why not)?
- Who is the best president you can remember? What was it that made him such a good president?
- Do you think that Mario Cuomo has been a good governor? Why (why not)?
- (Asked of those who had voted in a presidential election:) What qualities do you look for when you vote for president?
- (Asked of those who had voted in a congressional election:) What qualities do you look for when you vote for members of Congress?

- Are there any other people in politics today that you admire or think of as good politicians? (If yes:) Who is that, and why do you think of them that way?

Evaluations of the political system
- What do you think is the best thing about the American political system?
- What do you think is the worst thing about the American political system?
- What changes, if any, would you like to see in our political system?

Letter and reply form sent to potential subjects

This is the letter that was sent out to people chosen at random (through use of a random-number computer program) from the Utica telephone directory:

Date

Address

Dear (name),

I am an Assistant Professor of Government at Hamilton College who is working on a research project that is looking at how people think about politics. As part of that project, I would like to talk to an adult member of your household (I have chosen your name randomly from the Utica phone book).

I imagine the talk will last approximately 2 hours, and I am able to offer you $25 to compensate you for your time.

Please do not feel that you need to know anything about politics or care about politics to talk to me. I am interested in talking with as wide a group of people as possible, no matter how much or how little they think or care about politics.

I will record our talk, but what you say to me will be totally anonymous. No one but me will know the identities of the people I talk to.

The talk would occur at your convenience (morning, afternoon or evening) and can be held either in my office at the College or, if you prefer, in your home.

Please return the enclosed, self-addressed, stamped reply form to let me know whether or not an adult member of your household is willing to talk to me. If you are willing, I will call to make arrangements.

Thank you.

Sincerely,

ARTHUR SANDERS
Assistant Professor

This is the reply form that was included with a stamped envelope addressed to me at the college:

Name
Address

_____An adult member of this household is willing to talk. (Best time to phone to set up an appointment:_____.)

_____ No one is willing to talk.

Construction of variables from the 1984 American National Election Study

Style and policy orientation

The following are the numbers of the codes used to classify people in the 1984 American National Election Study as style- or policy-oriented. The codes are from the responses to the question of whether there was anything that the respondent liked or disliked about the Republican and Democratic parties (variables V267, V268, V269, V273, V274, V275, V279, V280, V281, V285, V286, V287). For a full description of the meaning of the codes see W. Miller and the National Election Studies, *American National Election Study, 1984* (Ann Arbor, Mich.: Inter-University Consortium for Political and Social Research, 1986), 653–73,n.3

STYLISTIC RESPONSES

1–508, 541–97, 601–4, 609–797, 802–4, 807–14, 831–97, 1010–12, 1102–3, 1201–97, 9996–7.

POLICY RESPONSES

509–36, 605–8, 801, 805–6, 815–30, 900–1009, 1013–1101, 1104–97.

Personality scale

Each respondent was told: "We'd like your impressions of Ronald Reagan (Walter Mondale). I am going to read a list of words and phrases people use to describe political figures. After each one, I would like you to tell me how much the word or phrase fits your impression of Ronald Reagan (Walter Mondale)."

The scale was created by adding 2 points for each answer of "a great deal," adding 1 point for each answer of "somewhat," subtracting 1 point for each answer of "a little," and subtracting 2 points for each answer of "not at all," creating a scale from 30 to −30. The fifteen characteristics were hardworking, decent, compassionate, commands respect, intelligent, moral, kind, inspiring, knowledgeable, good example, cares about people like you, good leadership, understands people like you, fair, in touch with ordinary people.

Issue closeness scale

This scale took the average distance that individuals saw between their position on a given issue and their perception of Reagan's (or Mondale's) position on the issue. Each question had a 7-point scale. The seven issues were the government services and spending trade-off (from "increase services and spending" to "decrease services and spending"); U.S. involvement in Central America; whether the government should guarantee each citizen a job and a decent standard of living or leave that up to the individual; whether government should aid minority groups; whether the government should help women; whether the United States should deal with the Russians by trying to cooperate more or by being tough; whether defense spending should be increased or decreased.

Retrospective evaluation scale

The responses to two questions were added together. The first question asked whether the individual approved or disapproved of the way Reagan was handling his job as president; it was scored from 1 for strong approval to 5 for strong disapproval. The second question was how good a job the government was doing in dealing with whatever problem the respondent had named as the most important problem facing the nation; it was scored 1 for good job, 3 for fair job, and 5 for poor job. Thus the scale ran from 2 for the most satisfied to 10 for the least satisfied.

Notes

Chapter 1

1. This interview was carried out in the summer of 1986, long before the Iran-Contra hearings made Central America an everyday topic for the news.

2. For the classic statement of this point, see P. Converse, "The Nature of Belief Systems in Mass Publics," in D. Apter, ed. *Ideology and Discontent* (New York: Free Press, 1964). For two good summaries of the state of our knowledge of public opinion, see D. Kinder and D. Sears, "Public Opinion and Political Action," in G. Lindzey and E. Aronson eds., *Handbook of Social Psychology,* 3d ed. (Reading, Mass.: Addison-Wesley, 1985); and P. Sniderman and P. Tetlock, "Interrelationship of Political Ideology and Public Opinion," in M. Hermann, ed., *Political Psychology* (San Francisco: Jossey-Bass, 1986). And for an exhaustive summary of the ways in which we can and should measure political sophistication, see R. Luskin, "Measuring Political Sophistication," *American Journal of Political Science* 31 (1987): 856–99.

3. For summaries of that literature, see Kinder and Sears, "Public Opinion"; Sniderman and Tetlock; and Luskin. Also see W. L. Bennett, "Perception and Cognition: An Information-Processing Framework for Politics," in S. Long, ed., *The Handbook of Political Behavior,* vol. 1 (New York: Plenum Press, 1981), which offers a more critical perspective on this literature.

4. Sniderman and Tetlock, 62.

5. R. E. Wolfinger, M. Shapiro, and F. I. Greenstein, *Dynamics of American Politics* (Englewood Cliffs, N.J.: Prentice-Hall, 1980).

6. F. I. Greenstein, and F. B. Feigert, *The American Party System and the American People,* 3d ed. (Englewood Cliffs, N.J.: Prentice-Hall, 1985).

7. The seminal piece is Converse.

8. Kinder and Sears, "Public Opinion," 664–71.

9. Ibid., 670.

10. Ibid., 671.

11. R. Lane, *Political Ideology: Why the American Common Man Believes What He Does* (New York: Free Press, 1962); and J. Hochschild, *What's Fair: American Beliefs About Distributive Justice* (Cambridge: Harvard University Press, 1981).

12. Lane, 350.

13. The interviews in this book were funded by grants from the American Political Science Association and Hamilton College.

14. See P. Sniderman with M. Hagen, *Race and Inequality* (Chatham, N.J.: Chatham House Publishers, 1985).

Chapter 2

1. See Converse; Kinder and Sears, "Public Opinion"; and Sniderman and Tetlock.

2. See Converse; and Kinder and Sears, "Public Opinion."

3. P. Conover and S. Feldman, "The Origins and Meaning of Liberal/Conservative Self-identifications," *American Journal of Political Science* 25 (1981): 617–45; and T. Levitan and W. Miller, "Ideological Interpretations of Presidential Elections," *American Political Science Review* 73 (1979): 751–71.

4. Conover and Feldman; Levitan and Miller; H. Brady and P. Sniderman, "Attitude Attribution: A Group Basis for Political Reasoning," *American Political Science Review* 79 (1985): 1061–78.

5. A. Campbell, P. Converse, W. Miller, and D. Stokes, *The American Voter* (New York: Wiley, 1960).

6. The literature on party identification is rich and complex. For overviews of this literature and the concept of party identification, see P. Abramson, *Political Attitudes in America* (San Francisco: W. H. Freeman and Co., 1983); S. Kamieniecki, *Party Identification, Political Behavior, and the American Electorate* (Westport, Conn.: Greenwood Press, 1985); and M. Wattenberg, *The Decline of American Political Parties, 1952–1984* (Cambridge: Harvard University Press, 1986).

7. A. Sanders, "The Meaning of Liberalism and Conservatism" *Polity* 19 (1986): 123–35.

8. Ibid.

9. See K. Knight, "Ideological Identification and the Content of the Ideological Agenda: 1960–1980," paper presented at the annual meeting of the American Political Science Association, Washington, D.C., 1984; and Sanders, "The Meaning of Liberalism."

10. Conover and Feldman, 641.

11. Ibid., 644.

12. P. Tetlock, "Cognitive Style and Political Ideology," *Journal of Personality and Social Psychology* 45 (1983): 118–25; and P. Tetlock, "Cognitive Style and Political Belief Systems in the British House of Commons," *Journal of Personality and Social Psychology* 46 (1984): 365–75.

13. These results fit quite nicely with the results I reported in a previous study (see Sanders, "The Meaning of Liberalism"). There I found that people with social-issue definitions of the term *conservative* displayed the highest correlations between their issue positions and their liberal-conservative self-placement within the issue area that they saw as relevant. On six out of seven social issues, the correlations for these individuals was above .53, with a maximum of .72. By comparison, on five economic issues, people with economic definitions of *conservative* displayed a correlation of .5 between their issue position and their self-placement on only one issue. (They did have higher correlations on economic issues than those with other types of definitions, but the levels of those correlations did not reach the levels of the correlations on social issues for people with social-issue definitions.)

14. For similar results using a national cross-section, see Sanders, "The Meaning of Liberalism."

15. One interesting difference that seems to emerge between my group of twenty-six and the national samples is the relatively small proportion of people I found with economic conceptions of these symbols. The coding that I did with the national samples that I examined in "The Meaning of Liberalism and Conservatism" and the coding done by Kathleen Knight in her paper "Ideological Identification and the Content of the Ideological Agenda: 1960–1980" both indicated a large proportion of economic responses. Knight

has suggested to me that this may be an artifact of the way the Center for Political Studies responses are coded. Many of the buzzwords that coders note (such as *thrifty, stingy, willing to spend money,* and so on) and thus code as a "spend-save" response may, in fact, be embedded within primarily stylistic responses. Because Knight has worked with the original interview protocols, I am grateful to her for pointing this out.

16. Tetlock, "Cognitive Style and Political Ideology"; and Tetlock, "Cognitive Style and Political Belief Systems."

17. If there was a single pattern present here, it was within the policy category, where those with social definitions were likely to use the labels in an evaluative way while those with economic definitions were not. This pattern matches the pattern of correlations I found in the 1980 American National Election Study; see Sanders, "The Meaning of Liberalism."

18. A. Sanders, "The Meaning of Party Image," *Western Political Quarterly* 41 (1988): 583–600.

19. Kinder and Sears, "Public Opinion," 673.

20. R. Trilling, *Party Image and Electoral Behavior* (New York: John Wiley and Sons, 1976).

21. Ibid., 88.

22. Chapter 4 of Trilling discusses the meaning of party images.

23. Wattenberg, 69.

24. D. Kinder, "Diversity and Complexity in American Public Opinion," in A. Finifter, ed., *Political Science: The State of the Discipline* (Washington, D.C.: American Political Science Association, 1983).

Chapter 3

1. The debate over the meaning of the decline in political trust began with A. Miller, "Political Issues and Trust in Government, 1964–1970," *American Political Science Review* 68 (1974): 951–72; J. Citrin, "Comment: The Political Relevance of Trust in Government," *American Political Science Review* 68 (1974):973–88; and A. Miller, "Rejoinder to 'Comment' by Jack Citrin: Political Discontent or Ritualism?" *American Political Science Review*

68 (1974): 989–1001. Also see J. Citrin, "The Changing American Electorate," in A. J. Meltsner, ed., *Politics and the Oval Office: Towards Presidential Governance* (San Francisco: Institute for Contemporary Study, 1981); A. Miller, E. Goldenberg, and L. Erbring, "Type-Set Politics: Impact of Newspapers on Public Confidence," *American Political Science Review* 73 (1979): 67–84; and P. Abramson and A. Finifter, "On the Meaning of Political Trust: New Evidence From Items Introduced in 1978," *American Journal of Political Science* 25 (1981): 297–307. For a good summary of the debate and the available evidence, see chapters 11–13 of Abramson. For a comprehensive look at this decline in trust and its implications, see S. M. Lipset and W. Schneider, *The Confidence Gap: Business, Labor, and Government in the Public Mind* (New York: Free Press, 1983).

2. I did not ask people if they supported the idea of limiting terms in government, so it may be that those with other trust orientations might endorse such an idea. It was not, however, important enough to others for them to raise the idea on their own.

3. These were not their real names.

4. These two orientations were coded at different times. When I was working on the attitudes toward trust, I did not have any written record in front of me describing each individual's liberal-conservative orientation, nor did I remember who fit in which category. It was only after I had almost completed the first draft of this chapter that I thought it might be useful to cross-tabulate these two orientations. I was genuinely surprised at how clear the relationship seemed to be and am therefore confident that my categorizing of trust attitudes was not in any way influenced by my categorizing of liberal-conservative orientation.

5. During the period of the interviews, the Tax Reform Act of 1986, which cut the number of rates to two, lowered taxes for most people, and eliminated a large number of deductions, was working its way through Congress. It had been introduced in the fall of 1985 and was passed by the House in December 1985 and by the Senate in June 1986. Over the summer and through the fall of 1986, it was considered by conference committee and then was sent in its final form to the House and the Senate. It was signed into law by the president in October. It had not yet passed by the time I finished the interviews, and it was a topic of discussion in the news

throughout the period I was interviewing people. Obviously, because the interviews were spread out over a four-month period, at times the topic was more prominent than at others. Thus, it would not be fair to draw strong conclusions based on whether people had heard of the bill, because some people clearly would have had an advantage in that area. However, the point of this discussion is that people's approach toward the bill (and tax reform in general) was influenced by their orientation toward trust. And it is reasonable, I think, to look at what people thought about tax reform from such an angle.

6. See Miller, "Political Issues"; Miller, "Rejoinder"; and Citrin, "Comment." Abramson also notes the need to better distinguish between these two kinds of trust in our measures. I would further add that we need to develop measures based on the interaction of these two independent types of trust rather than focus our attention on which type is declining or whether the trends we see represent a decline in trust in our leaders or in our system. Only a measure that distinguishes between and then combines these two types of trust will allow us to understand fully the implications of a decline (or rise) in trust and people's attitudes on these issues.

Chapter 4

1. This is not the real name of the street.

2. This does not mean that these groups did not use other sources. A few of those with local interests also watched the network newscasts, and some of those with national interests read the local papers. But those with national interests were much more likely to cite national sources as their major information source; those with local interests tended to cite local sources as their major source.

3. For the classic argument concerning the lack of knowledge about foreign-policy issues, see G. Almond, *The American People and Foreign Policy,* rev. ed. (New York: Praeger,1960); and J. Rosenau, *Public Opinion and Foreign Policy* (New York: Random House, 1961). Also see D. Devine, *The Attentive Public: Polyarchical Democracy* (Chicago: Rand McNally and Co.,1970); and Kinder and Sears, "Public Opinion."

Chapter 5

1. See Hochschild. Hochschild uses in-depth interviewing to get a fuller picture of how Americans make sense of equality in our society, and she discusses in great detail the ambivalence and confusion most people feel about such issues. I also found such ambivalence, which is discussed in Chapter 7. Here, however, I simply want to lay out the dominant patterns of values that people have. In this regard, people are usually relatively clear. It is when it comes to implementing these values that ambivalence arises, because people are not sure how to reach these goals, nor are they sure how to trade off the different values they are seeking when such trade-offs are necessary. Still, in making those trade-offs or in judging particular policies, the patterns of values that people have are important, even if the relationships among those values are not easy for them to discover.

2. For a fuller discussion of citizens' views of equality and justice, see Hochschild, an important work that sheds much light on how Americans grapple with politics in general and with issues of justice in particular. I do not think anything I found contradicts what Hochschild argues. The only real difference is in emphasis. I am interested here in how these values shape the way people make sense of politics, whereas she is interested in how people make sense of these issues of distributive justice.

3. This displeasure with the welfare system was one of the most commonly voiced complaints and is discussed more fully in Chapter 6.

4. This may also be the case with the other orientations, but the groups were too small to allow such a distinction to emerge. It was clear that none of the egalitarians thought equality had been achieved. In contrast, all of the libertarians seemed to think we had liberty, and that the problem was its erosion. The individualists seemed to think that although some tinkering might be needed, we had a great deal of opportunity here in the United States. With larger samples, it might be possible to distinguish more clearly people with these other three orientations by comparing their perceptions of the reality of the situation. Theoretically, at least, such perceptions should be as important in those categories as they were in the equality-of-opportunity category. An egalitarian who

thought equality had been achieved, for example, would probably have different views from those expressed by the egalitarians in this group.

Chapter 6

1. For attitudes toward busing, see D. Sears, C. Hensler, and L. Speer, "Whites' Opposition to Busing: Self-interest or Symbolic Politics," *American Political Science Review* 73 (1979): 369–84; and D. Kinder and D. Sears, "Prejudice and Politics: Symbolic Racism Versus Threats to the Good Life," *Journal of Personality and Social Psychology* 40 (1981): 414–31. For attitudes toward the economy, see D. Kinder and D. Kiewiet, "Economic Discontent and Political Behavior: The Role of Personal Grievances and Collective Economic Judgments in Congressional Voting," *American Journal of Political Science* 23 (1979): 495–527; and D. Kinder and D. Kiewiet, "Sociotropic Politics," *British Journal of Political Science* 11 (1981): 129–61; and D. Sears, R. Lau, T. Tyler, and A. Allen, "Self-interest Versus Symbolic Politics in Policy Attitudes and Presidential Voting," *American Political Science Review* 74 (1980): 670–84. For attitudes toward public spending, see A. Sanders, "Rationality, Self-Interest, and Public Attitudes on Public Spending," *Social Science Quarterly* 69 (1988): 311–24.

2. D. Sears and J. Citrin, *Tax Revolt: Something for Nothing in California* (Cambridge: Harvard University Press, 1982).

3. Some might argue that, in fact, this support of policies that are not in the individual's self-interest are, in fact, in that interest if one takes a broader view of self-interest. For example, supporting a tax increase might seem to be hurting an individual, but in the long run if such a policy brings prosperity to the nation, then it is in the individual's long-term self-interest. The problem with such a view is that *self-interest* loses all explanatory meaning. Any policy can be justified as being in someone's long-term self-interest on some grounds. If I support cutting spending on a program that helps me, it may strengthen the nation, and that in turn may help me. Thus, my motives may be not sociotropic, but selfish. But if that is true, self-interest becomes tautological. Everyone

supports policies that they think will be in their self-interest. They simply differ over whether short- or long-term self-interest is more important or over what is in one's self-interest. Clearly, all people act to help themselves at some level (even if it is only to feel better about themselves). If we take this broader view, then, self-interest loses any ability to serve as an analytical tool because it is always present. I think it is important, then, to restrict the meaning of *self-interest,* to define it in a narrow way. It seems to me that the best way to do that is to restrict *self-interest* to mean immediate tangible (material) self-interest. Any reasons for support that are nonmaterial or long-term should have a different name. (Here I call them conceptions of fairness.) This will allow us to distinguish between situations where self-interest is at work and situations where something else is the motivation.

4. See G. Kramer, "Short-term Fluctuations in U.S. Voting Behavior, 1896–1964," *American Political Science Review* 65 (1971): 131–43; E. Tufte, *Political Control of the Economy* (Princeton, N.J.: Princeton University Press, 1978); H. Bloom and H. D. Price, "Voter Response to Short-run Economic Conditions: The Asymmetric Effect of Prosperity and Recession," *American Political Science Review* 69 (1975): 1240–54; and S. Rosenstone, *Forecasting Presidential Elections* (New Haven, Conn.: Yale University Press, 1983). For studies showing limited self-interest effects at the individual level, see the references in notes 1 and 2 for this chapter. For a summary of this literature, see Kinder and Sears, "Public Opinion."

5. The people who expressed a desire for more fairness in the welfare system were Walter Beattie, Gail Blair, Al Chambliss, Adam Clay, Sue Doyle, Carl Figueroa, Howard Gossage, John Guidry, Bert Jackson, Mort Johnson, Clyde Lyle, Ralph Randolph, Laura Rivers, Ed Stanley, Dave Thomasson, Amy Tidrow, Carol Torrez, and Carla Zeber.

6. For a look at the effects of government performance on voting behavior, see V. O. Key, *The Responsible Electorate* (Cambridge: Harvard University Press, 1965); M. Fiorina, *Retrospective Voting in American National Elections* (New Haven, Conn.: Yale University Press, 1981); D. Kinder and W. Mebane, "Politics and Economics in Everyday Life," in K. Monroe, ed., *The Political Process and Economic Change* (New York: Agathon Press, 1983);

and D. Kiewiet, *Macroeconomics & Micropolitics* (Chicago: University of Chicago Press, 1983).

7. In that regard, it is interesting that a number of people took the questionnaires and letters they received from their representatives in Washington or Albany as evidence that these politicians were concerned with how their constituents felt about the issues. Simply having that contact gave them the experience (or perhaps illusion) of contact, which was taken as evidence of concern. Seven of the people I talked with mentioned these contacts, and in a positive manner. None of them was cynical about the meaning of the contacts. These contacts were also taken as a sign that the legislator was someone who was willing to listen, and this helped shape people's view of their legislator's style.

Chapter 7

1. See, for example, H. McClosky, P. J. Hoffman, and R. O'Hara, "Issue Conflict and Consensus Among Party Leaders and Followers," *American Political Science Review* 54 (1960): 406–27; S. A. Stouffer, *Communism, Conformity, and Civil Liberties* (New York: Doubleday, 1955); H. McClosky, "Consensus and Ideology in American Politics," *American Political Science Review* 58 (1964): 361–82; J. Sullivan, J. Piereson, and G. Marcus, "An Alternative Conceptualization of Political Tolerance: Illusory Increases 1950s–1970s," *American Political Science Review* 73 (1979): 781–94; J. Sullivan, J. Piereson, and G. Marcus, *Political Tolerance and American Democracy* (Chicago: University of Chicago Press, 1982); and H. McClosky and A. Brill, *Dimensions of Tolerance: What Americans Believe About Civil Liberties* (New York: Russell Sage Foundation, 1983). Although there is much debate over how tolerant the public is, the causes of tolerance, and whether tolerance (and belief in the ideals of democracy) has grown, there is agreement over the discrepency between people's abstract support for democratic principles and their willingness to ignore those principles in concrete cases.

2. Even such trust can be problematic. After Martha made her statement that if the president said it was okay, she would support it, I asked her if that meant she felt Congress should be

more willing to back the president. Her reply was that if Congress was not supportive, the legislators must have their reasons as well. And because she also trusted them, she was not sure they should have agreed to what the president wanted. Thus, Martha's willingness to trust our leaders did not really help her decide what to think about the issue, since the leaders she trusted had conflicting views.

Chapter 8

1. C. Gilligan, *In a Different Voice* (Cambridge: Harvard University Press, 1982).

2. Ibid., 156.

3. This gender gap may exist because the Democratic and Republican parties have stylistic images that fit this distinction. Republicans may be seen as a more macho party, while Democrats may be seen as a more compassionate party. Thus, more women may be Democrats not so much because of differences on issues as because of differences of style. Unfortunately, available survey data does not allow us to test this proposition.

4. For a similar discussion of the importance of understanding the meaning behind the opinions citizens express, see S. Rosenberg, "Reason and Ideology: Interpreting People's Understanding of American Politics," *Polity* 20 (1987): 114–44. Rosenberg's study focuses on what he calls the structure of thought, as he explores whether people relate their opinions in a sequential, linear or systematic style. My study looks at the content within these structures. It is possible that any of Rosenberg's structures could be primarily stylistic or primarily policy-oriented, and, thus, I think our work is complementary. What the two studies share is a concern for getting beyond a traditional "belief systems" approach and gaining a more complete understanding of how people actually reason about politics.

5. There were a maximum of twenty responses, five to each of the following questions: What do you like about the Democratic party? What do you dislike about the Democratic party? What do you like about the Republican party? What do you dislike about the Republican party?

6. For a discussion of the increasing numbers of people un-

able to think of anything they like or dislike about the parties, see Wattenberg; and Sanders, "The Meaning of Party Image."

7. The regressions were run with the feeling ratings, rather than vote choice, as the dependent variables for a number of reasons. First, feeling thermometers — scales running from one to a hundred — are better suited to ordinary least-squares regression analysis than are limited-choice variables such as vote choice. Second, my concern here was not to discover how people vote but to explore whether different people use different factors when evaluating candidates. Again, feeling thermometers seemed more important than vote choice. Third, using vote choice would have vastly complicated the issue variable, for then the direction of difference would have to be taken into account. People who were farther from Reagan than Mondale might not have been close to Mondale (and thus might not like him), but they might have liked Mondale better than Reagan. Thus, it was important to know if individuals placed themselves to the left or right of the candidates, as well as how far away they placed themselves. Looking at each candidate separately avoided that complication, because we would still expect closeness to affect feelings. Fourth, vote choice was strongly related to scores on the feeling thermometer. Well over 90 percent of the public voted for the candidate to whom they gave a higher thermometer reading. Thus, understanding how people evaluated candidates was important in understanding how they made their voting decision.

8. Only 4 percent gave Mondale a score of 30, and 0.5 percent gave him a score of −30. Six percent gave Reagan a score of 30, and 0.5 percent gave him a score of −30. Most individuals scored candidates somewhere between the two extremes, giving them more positive scores than negative scores. The mean score for Mondale was 10.5, with a standard deviation of 12.2. The mean score for Reagan was 10.3, with a standard deviation of 14.4.

9. The total number of respondents was 2,257. For Reagan, 148 people were missing, and the average issue distance was 1.9, with a standard deviation of 1.3. For Mondale, 225 people were missing, and the average distance was 1.7, with a standard deviation of 1.1.

10. I did not include series of questions on how people felt

about the way that Ronald Reagan was dealing with particular policy matters. Those questions were too specific for the purposes of this study. My interviews indicated that people use general evaluations to support their style decisions, not evaluations about specific policy. We might expect that policy-oriented individuals would be concerned with evaluating success in particular areas, but, as we have seen, they would not be particularly interested in general evaluations of success or failure.

11. The distinction between style and policy patterns was made with the preelection survey. On the other hand, all of the variables in the regressions were constructed from the postelection survey with the partial exception of the issue distance variable. (There were only three questions in the postelection survey, in which respondents were asked to place themselves and the candidates on an issues scale, as well, so I included four additional questions from the preelection survey.) By separating people into style and policy categories on the basis of the preelection survey and looking at regressions from the postelection survey, we minimize the chance that the differences in results for style- and policy-oriented people are simply a function of fleeting differences brought on by the survey itself. Whatever individuals were focusing on in their own minds on the day of the preelection survey would be unlikely to affect their answers a few months later. Thus, the differences between style- and policy-oriented individuals are likely to reflect something more substantial than passing thoughts.

12. In order to compare the effects of the same variable in different equations (Is personality more important for people with style patterns or for people with policy patterns?), one compares the actual coefficients. In order to look at the relative influence of the variables within any single equation (Are issues or retrospective evaluations more important for evaluations of Mondale by people with style patterns of thinking?), it is best to look at the standardized coefficient. There is, unfortunately, no simple way to look at the influence of different variables in different equations (such as, for example, the effect of party identification for Mondale as compared with the effect of issues for Reagan).

13. For similar findings, see C. Reinarman, *American States of Mind: Political Beliefs and Behavior Among Private and Public*

Workers (New Haven, Conn.: Yale University Press, 1987), especially chapters 4, 7, and 8. Reinarman used in-depth interviews with twelve people to explore differences in attitudes between public- and private-sector workers. He too found that people's experiences (combined with their values) were central in shaping political attitudes.

Bibliography

Abramson, P. *Political Attitudes in America*. San Francisco: W. H. Freeman and Co., 1983.

Abramson, P., and Finifter, A. "On the Meaning of Political Trust: New Evidence From Items Introduced in 1978." *American Journal of Political Science* 25 (1981): 297–307.

Almond, G. *The American People and Foreign Policy*. Rev. ed. New York: Praeger, 1960.

Bennett, W. L. "Perception and Cognition: An Information-Processing Framework for Politics." In *The Handbook of Political Behavior*, edited by S. Long, vol. 1. New York: Plenum Press, 1981.

Bloom, H., and H. D. Price. "Voter Response to Short-run Economic Conditions: The Asymmetric Effect of Prosperity and Recession." *American Political Science Review* 69 (1975): 1240–54.

Brady, H., and P. Sniderman. "Attitude Attribution: A Group Basis for Political Reasoning." *American Political Science Review*, 79 (1985): 1061–78.

Campbell, A., P. Converse, W. Miller, and D. Stokes. *The American Voter*. New York: Wiley 1960.

Citrin, J. "Comment: The Political Relevance of Trust in Government." *American Political Science Review* 68 (1974): 973–88.

_____. "The Changing American Electorate." In *Politics and the Oval Office: Towards Presidential Governance*, edited by A. J. Meltsner. San Francisco: Institute for Contemporary Study, 1981.

Conover, P., and S. Feldman. "The Origins and Meaning of Liberal/Conservative Self-identifications." *American Journal of Political Science* 25 (1981): 617–45.

Converse, P. "The Nature of Belief Systems in Mass Publics." In *Ideology and Discontent*, edited by D. Apter. New York: Free Press, 1964.

Devine, D. *The Attentive Public: Polyarchical Democracy*. Chicago: Rand McNally and Co.,1970.

Fiorina, M. *Retrospective Voting in American National Elections*. New Haven, Conn.: Yale University Press, 1981.

Gilligan, C. *In a Different Voice*. Cambridge: Harvard University Press, 1982.

Greenstein, F. I., and F. B. Feigert. *The American Party System and the American People.* 3d ed. Englewood Cliffs, N.J.: Prentice-Hall, 1985.

Hochschild, J. *What's Fair: American Beliefs About Distributive Justice.* Cambridge: Harvard University Press, 1981.

Kamieniecki, S. *Party Identification, Political Behavior, and the American Electorate.* Westport, Conn.: Greenwood Press, 1985.

Key, V. O. *The Responsible Electorate.* Cambridge: Harvard University Press, 1965.

Kiewiet, D. *Macroeconomics & Micropolitics.* Chicago: University of Chicago Press, 1983.

Kinder, D. "Diversity and Complexity in American Public Opinion." In *Political Science: The State of the Discipline,* edited by A. Finifter. Washington, D.C.: American Political Science Association, 1983.

Kinder, D., and D. Kiewiet. "Economic Discontent and Political Behavior: The Role of Personal Grievances and Collective Economic Judgments in Congressional Voting." *American Journal of Political Science* 23 (1979): 495–527.

———."Sociotropic Politics." *British Journal of Political Science* 11 (1981): 129–61.

Kinder, D., and W. Mebane, "Politics and Economics in Everyday Life." In *The Political Process and Economic Change*, edited by K. Monroe. New York: Agathon Press, 1983.

Kinder, D., and D. Sears. "Prejudice and Politics: Symbolic Racism Versus Threats to the Good Life." *Journal of Personality and Social Psychology* 40 (1981): 414–31.

———. "Public Opinion and Political Action." In *Handbook of Social Psychology, 3d ed.,* edited by G. Lindzey and E. Aronson. 3d ed., Reading, Mass.: Addison-Wesley, 1985.

Knight, K. "Ideological Identification and the Content of the Ideological Agenda: 1960–1980." Paper presented at the annual meeting of the American Political Science Association, Washington, D.C., 1984.

Kramer, G. "Short-term Fluctuations in U.S. Voting Behavior, 1896–1964." *American Political Science Review* 65 (1971): 131–43.

Lane, R. *Political Ideology: Why the American Common Man Believes What He Does.* New York: Free Press, 1962.

Levitan, T., and W. Miller. "Ideological Interpretations of Presidential Elections." *American Political Science Review* 73 (1979): 751–71.

Lipset, S. M., and W. Schneider. *The Confidence Gap: Business, Labor, and Government in the Public Mind.* New York: Free Press, 1983.

Luskin, R. "Measuring Political Sophistication." *American Journal of Political Science* 31 (1987): 856–99.

McClosky, H. "Consensus and Ideology in American Politics." *American Political Science Review* 58 (1964): 361–82.

McClosky, H., and A. Brill. *Dimensions of Tolerance: What Americans Believe About Civil Liberties.* New York: Russell Sage Foundation, 1983.

McClosky, H., P. J. Hoffman, and R. O'Hara. "Issue Conflict and Consensus Among Party Leaders and Followers." *American Political Science Review* 54 (1960): 406–27.

Miller, A. "Political Issues and Trust in Government, 1964–1970." *American Political Science Review* 68 (1974): 951–72.

_____. "Rejoinder to 'Comment' by Jack Citrin: Political Discontent or Ritualism?" *American Political Science Review* 68 (1974): 989–1001.

Miller, A., E. Goldenberg, and L. Erbring. "Type-Set Politics: Impact of Newspapers on Public Confidence." *American Political Science Review* 73 (1979): 67–84.

Reinarman, C. *American States of Mind: Political Beliefs and Behavior Among Private and Public Workers.* New Haven, Conn.: Yale University Press, 1987.

Rosenau, J. *Public Opinion and Foreign Policy.* New York: Random House, 1961.

Rosenberg, S. "Reason and Ideology: Interpreting People's Understanding of American Politics." *Polity* 20 (1987): 114–44.

Rosenstone, S. *Forecasting Presidential Elections.* New Haven, Conn.: Yale University Press, 1983.

Sanders, A. "The Meaning of Liberalism and Conservatism." *Polity* 19 (1986): 123–35.

_____. "Rationality, Self-interest, and Public Attitudes on Public Spending." *Social Science Quarterly* 69 (1988): 311–24.

_____. "The Meaning of Party Image." *Western Political Quarterly,* 41 (1988): 588–600.

Sears, D., and J. Citrin. *Tax Revolt: Something for Nothing in California.* Cambridge: Harvard University Press, 1982.

Sears, D., C. Hensler, and L. Speer. "Whites' Opposition to Busing: Self-interest or Symbolic Politics." *American Political Science Review* 73 (1979): 369–84.

Sears, D., R. Lau, T. Tyler, and A. Allen. "Self-interest Versus Symbolic Politics in Policy Attitudes and Presidential Voting." *American Political Science Review* 74 (1980): 670–84.

Sniderman, P. with M. Hagen. *Race and Inequality.* Chatham, N.J.: Chatham House Publishers, 1985.

Sniderman, P., and P. Tetlock. "Interrelationship of Political Ideology and Public Opinion." In *Political Psychology,* edited by M. Hermann. San Francisco: Jossey-Bass, 1986.

Stouffer, S. A. *Communism, Conformity, and Civil Liberties.* New York: Doubleday, 1955.

Sullivan, J., J. Piereson, and G. Marcus. "An Alternative Conceptualization of Political Tolerance: Illusory Increases 1950s–1970s." *American Political Science Review* 73 (1979): 781–94.

_____. *Political Tolerance and American Democracy.* Chicago: University of Chicago Press, 1982.

Tetlock, P. "Cognitive Style and Political Ideology." *Journal of Personality and Social Psychology* 45 (1983): 118–25.

_____. "Cognitive Style and Political Belief Systems in the British House of Commons." *Journal of Personality and Social Psychology* 46 (1984): 365–75.

Trilling, R. *Party Image and Electoral Behavior.* New York: John Wiley and Sons, 1976.

Tufte, E. *Political Control of the Economy.* Princeton, N.J.: Princeton University Press, 1978.

Wattenberg, M. *The Decline of American Political Parties, 1952–1984.* Cambridge: Harvard University Press, 1986.

Wolfinger, R. E., M. Shapiro, and F. I. Greenstein. *Dynamics of American Politics.* Englewood Cliffs, N.J.: Prentice-Hall, 1980.

Index